The Book on Personal Development

How to Legally Boost Your Income

And Drastically Improve Your Intelligence

Other books by Dan Christian Yeung:

Dealership Deceit

Save Money, Build Wealth

The Book On Project Management

How To Keep Your Job If You Think You're About To Lose It

The Book On Personal Development

How to Legally Boost Your Income
And Drastically Improve Your Intelligence

Dan Christian Yeung

DanChristianYeung.com

Copyright © 2017 by Dan Christian Yeung

All Rights Reserved. No part of this book may be reproduced, transmitted, or distributed in any form or by any means, electrical or mechanical, including photocopying and recording, or by any information storage or retrieval system without permission in writing from the Author.

ISBN: 978-0-9947715-2-0

Published by 10-10-10 Publishing, Markham, ON Canada

The information contained in this book is provided *as is*, without warranty of any kind. The entire risk as to the results and the performance of the information is assumed by the user, and in no event shall the Author be liable for any consequential, incidental, or direct damages suffered in the course of using the information in this book.

To my wife, Thy, and my daughter, Rachel.

Table of Contents

Introduction 11

Section One: Reprogram Your Mind 15

Reprogram Your Mind 17

Why I Have Such a Weird Message on the Home Screen of My Phone 21

How to Get Anything You Want in Life: Pretend You Already Have It 27

Section Two: Things Successful People Do 33

What Successful People Do Differently Than the Rest of Us 35

You Don't Have to Become the Next Bill Gates to be Successful 39

This Secret Only Works If You're Doing What You Love 43

Why Rich People Don't Need Broken Ice 47

Successful People Spend 90% of Their Time Doing This 51

Here's How Most Successful People Got to Where They Are 57

Here's What Successful People Focus Most of Their Time and Energy On 63

Get the Life You Want by Answering This Simple Little Question 69

Section Three: Overcoming Rejection 75

Why You Need to Treat Negative Feedback as a Gift 77

Don't Let This Stop You From Fulfilling Your Life Mission 83

Section Four: Boost Your Self-Esteem 87

The 5-Minute Phobia Cure 89
The Power of Celebrating Even the Tiniest of Successes 95
How to Boost Your Self-Esteem Using Eye Contact 99
Boost Your Self-Esteem With This Bizarre Exercise 101

Section Five: Overcoming Frustration and Anger 107

How to Release Yourself From Feelings of Frustration and Anger 109

Section Six: Money 117

How to Earn More Money Without Getting a Raise or Working More Hours 119

This Message Could be Worth $3000 to You (Especially if You're a Landscaper) 123

The Middle Class is Disappearing: Make Sure Your Money Doesn't Follow Suit 129

The Ancient Babylonians Were a Very Wealthy Race: Want to Know Their Secret? 135

Why You Always Have a Choice (Even When It Feels Like You Don't) 139

The SWAT Team and Your Life Mission 143

Section Seven: Goal-Setting and Achievement 149

How to Achieve Any Goal You Set for Yourself 151

How to Get Motivated to Do Something You Don't Feel Like Doing 157

The Rule of 5: How to Get Huge Tasks Done Faster Than You Think 161

How an 81-Year-Old Bob Proctor Can Still Crush It Onstage Like He's 20 165

Success Leaves Clues — Do You Know How to Find Them? 169

Why You Can't Go at It Alone 173

Are You Still on Track? 177

How to Navigate Through Tough, Life-Altering Decisions .. 181

What Would Your Life Look Like if You Asked Yourself These Three Questions? 185

Section Eight: Productivity 189

How to Conduct a Powerful and Productive Meeting 191

Why You Can't Manage Time but You *CAN* Manage This ... 197

How to Make It Harder for Your Boss to Lay You Off 201

How to Find an Extra Seven Hours a Week of Free Time ... 205

Why Working on Your Weaknesses is a Waste of Time 209

You *DO* Have the Time — You're Just Choosing to Waste It 215

Impress Potential Clients With This Memory Hack 221

How to Make Your Memory 100x Sharper 225

Conclusion 231

Introduction

Snowmen fall to earth, unassembled.

There are literally billions of people running around the world right now with the following thought in their mind:

"There's nothing special about me. I'm just an average human being."

I think we've all thought this at one point or another.

But, here's the thing:

Nothing could possibly be *FURTHER* from the truth!

You are a *VERY* special person. You are one-of-a-kind. You have *TONS* of experience which will benefit many other people. By this I mean you have stories and experiences inside of you which other people desperately need to hear.

How do I know this?

Simple. You're the only person on this planet who has lived the life you've lived. You're the only person on this planet who's experienced what you've experienced.

Even if you think or feel you've lived a very normal life, you're the only one who's lived it. You're the only one who's achieved what you've achieved, and you're the only one who's overcome the obstacles and pains you've had to overcome.

We all have so much to offer. We all have a story to tell and we all have experiences to share which will enrich the lives of those who hear them, and you are no exception — this includes *your* story.

Even my 7-month-old daughter, Rachel, has value to offer. She's still learning how to crawl, mind you, and yet she's already managed to teach me a few things about life!

Here are a few things Rachel has taught me:

1) You don't get better at flipping over by crying and screaming. You get better at flipping over by *actually flipping over* (and over, and over, and over).

2) It's much easier to get others to do what you want them to do by being happy and cute than by being bratty and whiny.

3) If you're bored with a toy, put it down and find something else to play with. There's no point forcing yourself to play with something you don't want to play with.

4) You can find joy in almost anything, no matter how small or insignificant it may seem to others.

5) You're not going to know if a toy is fun to play with until you *actually play with it*.

6) If you want something, let someone else know! If you can't get it yourself, ask someone to get it for you. Or, in Rachel's case, point at it and make cute noises. Don't just hope someone will be able to read your mind and know what you want. You'll be disappointed and frustrated.

Now, that's not to say you'll get that thing, necessarily, but it's better to ask and be told "no" than it is to never have asked at all.

7) Babies don't make any prejudicial distinctions between black, white, Asian, male, female, gay, straight, fat, skinny, ugly, beautiful, etc. until we condition them to do so.

All this from a 7-month-old!

If an infant can teach me — and you — this much about life, surely you can think of something of value *you* can offer others, especially as a potential mentor.

Keep this in mind the next time you catch yourself thinking there's nothing special about you.

It's the most inaccurate statement you can make.

Section One: Reprogram Your Mind

Reprogram Your Mind

Live a life of abundance and wealth by planting these "seeds" in your mind . . .

One morning, while we were waiting in line to get coffee, a friend of mine asked me how I was doing.

I replied, "Wonderful! How about you?"

He responded, "You're always wonderful! Even if it's raining or snowing outside, or even if you're having problems with your clients. Why is that?"

It's simple. Actually, the reason can be traced back to the Bible.

The following verse can be found in *Galatians 6:7, KJV*:

"for whatsoever a man soweth, that shall he also reap."

If I were to start complaining and to start spreading negativity, I would attract more negativity into my life. Soon, the Universe would start giving me more things to be negative about.

By the same token, if I spread feelings of happiness and gratitude — no matter what's going on in my physical environment — I will attract more things to be happy and grateful for.

Here's another fact about sowing and reaping:

There's a season to sow, and there's a season to reap, but:

You don't do both in the same season!

Farmers know this all too well. Farmers know that you *HAVE* to work hard and plant as many of the best seeds as you can find during the sowing season. How hard you work and the quality of your seeds determine how much bounty you will be able to secure during the season of reaping.

If you don't plant a lot of seeds, the seeds you do plant are of poor quality, or you don't make an effort to do a good job sowing, there's not going to be too much to reap when the time comes.

So how does this apply to you?

Well, you're always planting "seeds" in your mind. This is happening whether you're aware of it or not. The good news is that you get to choose what seeds get planted in your mind.

If you hang out with negative people and you watch a lot of negative television — the news, for instance — you'll plant negative seeds in your mind. When those seeds germinate, your mind will become full of negative and limiting beliefs. These beliefs will play a large part in preventing you from getting the income and lifestyle you want.

On the other hand, if you hang out with positive people and spend your time learning new skills, improving your self-esteem, and learning how to be even more grateful for what you already have, you'll have a beautiful and creative mind. You'll believe you can achieve anything you want — which is true by the way — and you'll easily discover how to reach that goal.

So, try to focus on planting as many positive seeds in your mind as possible. You can do this by restricting the amount of time you spend consuming negative media and the time you spend with negative people and, instead, spend that time with positive people and consuming uplifting books and programs.

But, don't expect an immediate change. You have to keep at it for a while — the Season of Sowing — before you can obtain the benefits — the Season of Reaping.

I know it's tough to do, especially when you don't see the resulting benefits right away. But, keep at it. Trust me. Every seed has a germination period — keep planting positive ones, and eventually you'll discover how to get the income and lifestyle you've always wanted.

Why I Have Such a Weird Message on the Home Screen of My Phone

I have the following message on the home screen of my phone:

By May 31, 2019, I am so happy and grateful now that I have a net worth of $1,558,687.

Lots of people have asked me why I have such a "weird message" there.

Here's the reason: It's an affirmation.

An affirmation is simply a statement of truth.

Now, it may not be true in the physical world. At least, not yet.

Our minds are a very powerful thing. There are a lot of things that we have the ability to do, even though we're not consciously thinking about them.

Like, do you know how to pump blood around your body? Do you know how to process food and turn it into usable energy? Well, we're doing it all the time so we *must* know how. But we don't consciously know how to do it. Our subconscious mind knows how, and *it* does it. All the time.

The secret to getting anything you want, at least according to most spiritual thinkers, is to convince your subconscious mind that you already have it.

Your subconscious mind already knows how to achieve any goal your conscious mind can set. You just need some way of getting your subconscious mind to reveal it.

And two of the most powerful ways of getting your subconscious mind to believe that you have already achieved your goal in the physical world are through affirmation and visualization.

Every time you tell your subconscious mind that something is true, it believes it and works toward making it true in the physical world.

But, here's the thing:

Every thought you think and every word you say is an affirmation.

So, be very careful about what you think and what you say. Saying negative words out loud and thinking negative thoughts in your mind can bring about negative events in your physical world.

But how do you create a proper affirmation?

Different spiritual teachers will tell you different ways of creating them, but I'll show you how I do it. My method is a hybrid of the teachings of Bob Proctor and Jack Canfield:

1) Start with writing down a future target date.
2) Write, "I am so."
3) Write a positive-feeling word — happy, grateful, uplifted, courageous, etc.
4) Write "now that" — it *HAS* to be in present tense because we're trying to convince our subconscious mind that you've already achieved your goal.
5) Write down your goal.

Your goal can't have negative connotations in it. For example, you can't say "I'm so happy and grateful that

I'm no longer in debt." Your subconscious mind doesn't have the ability to interpret negative associations or undertones such as this. The words "don't" and "no longer" don't mean anything to it.

Here's an illustration: I do not want you to think about pink elephants. At all. Do not think about pink elephants.

What are you thinking about right now?

Exactly.

If your goal is to stop smoking, be happy and grateful now that you're breathing clean air. If your goal is to get out of debt, be happy and grateful now that you have multiple streams of real-estate income.

Also, it has to be about you. You can't really affirm the actions of someone else — you can only affirm your own thoughts and actions.

Example: I'm so happy and grateful now that my son is cleaning his room

Correct: I'm so happy and grateful now that I'm coaching my son to clean his room.

Lastly, try to be as specific as possible.

Try to come up with an affirmation using these guidelines. When you do, and when you're in a safe place by yourself, try to say them to yourself at least 100 times while visualizing yourself in possession of your goal.

Or, you can do what I do and keep them written down in a place where you'll see them at least 100 times a day. That way, they'll be ingrained into your subconscious mind.

Keep in mind, some of the richest as most successful people in the world — think Oprah Winfrey — do this on a regular basis.

If someone thinks you're "weird" for doing this, take a look at where they are in life. If your goal is to be just like them, then take their advice.

But, remember, even professional athletes do this all the time. Think about sprinters at the starting line just before they run a race. Think about gymnasts or figure skaters just before they start their routine. Think about football players right before they hit the field.

What do you think they're thinking about?

I'll bet you that most of them are thinking about that race they just won. Or that routine they aced. Or that big catch or sack they just made.

If you keep this up for 30 days, you'll be surprised to find how much closer you are to achieving your goal.

How to Get Anything You Want in Life: Pretend You Already Have It

Here's a question I tend to get asked quite a lot:

"Dan, why are you always wearing a suit?"

It's a good question. Why *AM* I always wearing a suit?

Simple. I'm acting as if I'm already running a $10M-a-year personal-development company.

But, why am I pretending to do something I'm not yet actually doing?

As you probably already know, if you want to get to where you want to go, you've got to start acting like you're *already there*.

You have to act AS IF.

This is Principle #12 in Jack Canfield's best-seller, *The Success Principles*.

If you want to be an Olympic gold medalist, you've got to act as if you've already won the event. What do you think's going on in each and every sprinter's mind right before they get into the starting blocks? That's right, they're already running the race — and winning it! — in their minds.

Everything's done twice. First it's done in the mind, and then it's done in real life.

There's no such thing as an "original painting." Every painting you'll ever see is a replication. The "original" can only ever be found in the mind of the artist.

Michelangelo first saw his paintings of the Sistine Chapel in his mind before he picked up his brush. Mozart, Beethoven, and Bach all *FIRST* heard their symphonies and concertos in their minds before transcribing their beautiful music onto paper.

That's why I'm always wearing a suit. I'm seeing myself already in possession of what I want in life. I want to be a high-ticket speaker, trainer, and coach. High-ticket speakers, trainers, and coaches wear suits all the time. So, it makes sense that I wear a suit all the time as well.

Tony Robbins is famous for saying, "Success leaves clues."

See what successful people do, and then emulate them.

Case in point:

Most of the male tellers at the bank I go to wear a dress shirt and dress pants. But, there was this one teller who *ALWAYS* wore a suit and tie.

After several months, I noticed him sitting in the manager's office.

I asked him what had happened. He said he'd gotten promoted to Manager.

Why? Was it because of his qualifications? Not entirely. Certainly, he was qualified. But, he likely had the same qualifications as all the other tellers who'd applied.

In large part, it was because everyone that didn't know him very well assumed he already *WAS* a manager.

He acted and dressed like the other managers at the bank. The managers at the bank loved to golf, so he learnt how to golf. And so on. By the time a management position had opened up, everyone realized he was a natural fit.

You've got to act AS IF!

I can't say this enough.

If you're looking for a special man or woman in your life, but you've got so much junk on your bed you barely have room for *yourself,* clean your bed! Make room for your future partner — both in your mind and on your bed!

You know the old adage, "You've gotta fake it 'til you make it"? Well, guess what? It's true.

Want to know why there was a *HUGE* mural of the Moon in the room the scientists occupied while they were working on getting Neal Armstrong there?

Everyone was acting as if we'd already done it!

The question wasn't whether we *could* do it, the question was HOW.

I'm giving you the formula for success right here. Get over the awkwardness and start acting like you're already successful. See yourself in your mind as already having achieved the lifestyle and income you want.

That's why I'm so big on affirmations, visualization, meditation, and vision boards.

Note: A vision board is a visual aid, such as a collage of images pinned to a cork board, placed so that you can see it every day. It's basically your affirmations in visual form.

Your subconscious mind is much more powerful than you know. It can pretty much get you anything you want. The thing is, it can't reject commands or suggestions like your conscious mind can. That's why if you keep putting negative thoughts in your conscious mind, they'll seep through to your subconscious mind and they'll eventually become true in your physical world as a result.

If you put thoughts in your mind such that you've already accomplished a goal — a goal you've already realized in your mind but want to manifest in your physical world as well — your subconscious mind will work to that end, to make that a reality.

What more can I say? Act *as if*. If you keep it up long enough, it'll eventually become true.

Section Two: Things Successful People Do

What Successful People Do Differently Than the Rest of Us

Why should we talk about habits? Well, 95% of what we do as human beings is habitual.

Think about it.

You probably wake up at the exact same time every day. You probably do the exact same things in the washroom in the exact same order as well. I'm also willing to bet you take the exact same route to work each and every morning.

We love habits. Our habits and rituals help us feel comfortable.

I've talked a lot about success, and I can tell you the #1 difference between the successful people and the not-so-successful people are their habits and the small things they do on a daily basis.

We all have habits. It's just that successful people have different habits than the rest of us.

Actually, why don't I give you a list of some of my daily habits which have helped me get to where I am right now:

- Every morning, when I wake up, I look for things to be grateful for — things like the clean air in my house and the beautiful trees right outside my window.
- I thank God for giving me the family and life I have, and the opportunity to do what I love.
- I review my monthly goals.
- I do an accountability call.
- I post something of value for you on Facebook.
- I write an email or post.
- Every night, before I go to sleep, I look at myself in the mirror. I compliment myself for anything I've accomplished that day. Then I tell myself I

love myself. This exercise has done wonders for my psyche as well as my self-esteem. In order to accomplish huge goals and do big things, you need to have loads of self-esteem.

- o Before I fall asleep, I visualize myself living my ideal life. I've noticed that I tend to dream about my last thought, so ensuring my last thoughts are about becoming the person I want to become goes a long way to programming my subconscious mind to believe I've already achieved my Big Hairy Audacious Goal.

So, here's my question to you: What are some of your habits? Now, which of those are getting you towards the health, income, and lifestyle you've always wanted?

If the answer is "none," don't worry! You're in the vast majority.

Think of a habit or two you would like to establish that will get you to where you want to go. Maybe you want to get into the habit of posting a daily video. Maybe you want to get into the habit of reviewing your monthly goals on a daily basis. Maybe you want to start meditating and/or repeating affirmations to yourself each and every morning.

Pick a few and establish them. Do them every day for at least 30 days. Don't skip a day! If you do, you have to start over. Get your accountability partner — a person who coaches another person in terms of helping the other person keep a commitment — to help you if need be.

Successful people tend to have different habits and rituals than the rest of us. They tend to do things such as repeat affirmations, meditate, and visualize on a daily basis.

If you want to become successful, consider incorporating success habits into your daily routine.

You Don't Have to Become the Next Bill Gates to be Successful

I often mention to my coaching clients that success is nothing but a 7-Step Formula. However, a lot of them have a tough time believing me.

See, the thought of becoming the next Bill Gates or the next Steve Jobs is daunting, and scary as hell.

But, here's the thing: I'm not asking you to become the next Bill Gates. Or the next Steve Jobs.

Actually, I would really prefer it if you didn't. There's already a Mark Zuckerberg, Bob Proctor, and an Oprah Winfrey. The world doesn't need another of any of these, specifically.

You don't have to be a billionaire, for instance. I use money when I talk about success because that's what success looks like to most people. Most people tie success to how much money you can make.

But, really, success is the progressive realization of a worthy ideal. In simpler terms, you're successful when you figure out what it is you actually want out of life and you start chipping away at it.

You really want to be a plumber, say, but you're working as a carpenter? Then you're not successful — at least not yet. You start becoming successful only once you begin taking plumbing courses and practicing the craft.

If you put away your plumbing stuff, you stop being successful.

Make sense?

You can still be successful only making $10,000 a month.

What's your ideal income?

You don't have to be a billionaire for the sake of being a billionaire. If your ideal life consists of two beachfront houses, a Porsche, and the ability to build a hospital in Africa, you don't need a billion dollars. I don't think you even need $10M.

The pursuit of money alone is an empty one. If that's your goal, you'll live a sad and lonely life and there's a pretty good chance no one will show up at your funeral.

Accumulate enough wealth to buy the stuff you want to buy, but also express appreciation and gratitude. End human suffering. Make the world a better place. Focus on that.

You'll find you won't need as much money as you think.

By the way, you can grab your copy of the 7-Step Formula at *DanChristianYeung.com*.

This Secret Only Works If You're Doing What You Love

Success is hard work. Making tons of money and getting the lifestyle you want is hard work. It doesn't come easy.

And I know I say this over and over, but, at least in my opinion, it's a message you can't hear enough:

If you're doing what you hate, life will be tough. You won't enjoy the work. Your heart won't be in it. You will be in a position where you can't wait to quit.

If you're doing what you love, however, life will almost seem magical. You can't wait to set to work. You'll *LOVE* the work. Your whole heart will be in it.

As you likely know if you're reading these very words, I

just released my third book: *The Book on Personal Development*. You're holding it in your hands, of course, and I thank you for that.

But, you know what's weird about this particular book? It's been by far the easiest for me to write.

I've written two books before this one. I enjoyed the process of writing them both. But, toward the end of each, I had to physically force myself to sit down and actually finish them.

However, with *The Book on Personal Development*, I just couldn't stop working on it! Writing this book has got to be one of the most enjoyable things I've ever done!

Why?

Because writing The Book on Personal Development *is on course with my life mission.*

Personal Development is what I want to do. It's who I am. I want to spend my life and my energy helping you overcome *HUGE* obstacles and get the life you want. Outside of my family, there's nothing else more exciting to me in the world than this.

You'll be in a much better position to improve the lives of others if you use and exploit your gifts and talents. In return, you'll be richly rewarded with the money needed in order to get the lifestyle you've always wanted.

Bob Proctor once said:

"If you don't have money, the amount of good you can do is limited to how much time you have."

The pursuit of money isn't evil — no matter what some might say — because, after all, you can't build hospitals and shelters without money.

The secret to life is simple. Be grateful for what you have. Use your talents to make the world a better place. Show appreciation and gratitude by giving back.

This only works if you're doing what you love.

Why Rich People Don't Need Broken Ice

I visit the gym every day for about an hour or so. There's a TV in the locker room, and it's usually set to a 24-hour news channel. There are also a few recliners situated around the TV — which seems counter-intuitive for a gym.

When I got to the gym one particular day, all the recliners were occupied by guys watching coverage of a massive forest fire. The guys were staring in shock as they saw image after image of fires and houses burning down.

I went for my hour-long run, and when I came back into the locker room, the same guys were still sitting there watching the same thing! They'd stared at the TV for an hour, watching the same repeating coverage of the fire over and over again.

But, here's a question: What do you think the effect of watching repetitive negative news coverage has on your thinking and your self-esteem?

You're just imprinting your subconscious mind with images of houses and forests burning down. Doing this will kill your self-esteem because you're going to end up spending most of your time and mental energy focusing on the people that are affected and the fire itself.

If you feel bad for the people affected by the fire, there are a few ways you could help in this scenario: If you're in Northern Alberta, you could volunteer to help out with the rescue effort. Otherwise, you could donate money to the Red Cross.

Sitting in front of the TV and feeling bad for the people affected by the fire, though, unfortunately won't help them. All it does is generate more anxiety for you and lower your self-esteem.

A lot of successful people I know, including *The New York Times* best-selling authors Raymond Aaron and Tim Ferriss, don't even watch the news.

If you want a surefire way to improve your self-esteem:

Stop watching the news.

Most of it is negative.

Actually, believe it or not, the news is for broke people. Here's why: Is 90% of the population rich or broke? As you know, the answer is "Broke." Now, is the news catered towards 90% of the population or 10% of the population? There you go.

Instead of watching the news or reading the paper, I'd suggest downloading podcasts or watching videos produced by trainers and gurus with a positive message. I love personal development so I'm always listening to Jack Canfield and Bob Proctor, but lately I'm trying to improve my marketing and business skills so I'm spending at least a few hours a day listening to *ilovemarketing.com* podcasts.

Spending three hours a day listening to self-help and marketing audios has gotten me further ahead in the last 6 months than spending three hours a day watching the news over the last 20 years.

So, here's my suggestion for you: Try this out. Try to not watch the news for seven days. Instead, spend the time listening to podcasts or watching YouTube videos produced by people with a positive message.

If you don't notice an improvement in your mood and your thinking, then go back to what you were doing before. But, I'm willing to bet that your self-esteem and your mood will dramatically improve once you stop paying attention to the news.

Successful People Spend 90% of Their Time Doing This

What are you doing this weekend? If you're like most people, you probably have a huge list of chores you need to get done such as: vacuuming, cleaning, tidying up the house, mowing the lawn, weeding the garden, fixing the flat tire on your kid's bicycle, etc.

There's always a ton of stuff we need to get done both at home and at work. Some of these tasks require us to use our core genius — in other words, what we love to do or what we're really good at doing. Other tasks could very well be done by a monkey — albeit a very clever monkey — but we still have to get them done ourselves, as hiring a monkey is not always practical.

Here's the thing though: As you know, I've spent a lot of time trying to figure out what makes successful people, well, successful.

The truth is that successful people aren't that different from the rest of us. However, what makes successful people successful is, among other things, how they go about getting their stuff done.

Once you become aware you've got to get something done — wash the dishes, clean the floor, do your taxes — you have four options:

1. Do it right away.
2. Delay it.
3. Dump it.
4. Delegate it.

Most of us are pretty good at 1, 2, and 3. We're good at doing stuff right away ... *cough* ... , putting it off and doing it at a later time, or getting rid of the task altogether if someone else did it for us or if the deadline passed and we don't need to do it anymore.

But, what differentiates successful people from the rest of us?

Successful people spend 90% of their time and energy exercising their core genius. They DELEGATE the rest to others.

You see, most of us are only really good at a few things. Some of us are good at small-business accounting. Others are good at structural engineering. People such as myself are good at personal development and buying cars at dealerships. But very few of us are good at accounting *AND* vacuuming *AND* mowing the lawn *AND* buying cars at dealerships.

You'll never see Bill Gates mow his own lawn. You'll never see Richard Branson fix his own airplanes.

Why? Because they have a lot of money so they can afford a landscaper and a mechanic?

That is true, but that's not the main reason.

They don't do it because they're not good at it. Richard and Bill are good at starting businesses and making deals, not mowing the lawn. Landscapers are good at mowing lawns, so Richard and Bill leave that task to them.

Successful people only do what they're good at and what they love to do. They delegate the rest.

"But I can't afford that!"

I can hear your thoughts all the way from here.

There are ways to pay little to nothing for a cleaner, accountant, or housekeeper:

1) Hire people cheaply on Craigslist and Kijiji.

2) Barter. Assuming you love accounting but you hate cleaning your house, find someone on Craigslist or Kijiji or even at a networking event, and offer to do some accounting for them in exchange for their cleaning services. That person may love cleaning but hate accounting.

3) Let's say you get paid $20 per hour. Let's also say that a cleaning company costs $15 per hour. What's more efficient for you? Clean your house, or hire someone for $15 per hour while you're out there earning $20 per hour at the same time (hopefully exercising your core genius)?

4) Use a virtual assistant. I hired mine through *taskbullet.com*, and she only costs about $5 per hour. Any task you do not want to do that can be done online — such as doing your taxes, booking doctor's appointments, looking for and buying gifts, booking vehicle service, sending thank-you cards,

accounting and book keeping, etc. — should be done through a virtual assistant. VA companies such as TaskBullet have college-educated employees — they have full-blown degrees and have engineering and accounting accreditation — that are completely fluent in English.

Does this mean you should delegate every single task right now other than the few that are part of your core genius?

Well, no. But you should take a look at all the tasks you do on a regular basis and see which ones you can get someone such as a VA to do for you.

So, here's your homework: First, make a list of tasks that you need to do. Next, see which ones you like doing and which ones you don't like doing. After that, take a look at the tasks you don't like doing and separate out those which could be done over the internet.

Next, visit *taskbullet.com* and take a look at the services they have to offer. You don't have to hire them or anything right now — just take a look.

But, trust me, hiring a VA completely changed my life. I no longer have to worry about tracking bills, buying and selling stocks, buying birthday and anniversary presents, sending out reminder emails to my floor hockey team, doing my taxes, or booking doctor's appointments.

Here's How Most Successful People Got to Where They Are

I took my buddy out for coffee the other day. He currently works for the government, but he *HATES* his job. They don't give him a lot of responsibility. Despite being an engineer, he's only given administrative tasks by his supervisor.

We talked for a while and it turns out he actually doesn't want to be an engineer at all. He'd rather own a landscaping or surveying company.

Interesting.

I asked him what he's doing right now to get himself towards that goal.

He said, "Nothing."

And, you know what, that's typical. Most of us have jobs we don't like doing, and know what we'd rather be doing instead. But, not many of us actually start working towards making our dream job a reality.

He went on to tell me how hard it is to start a company and how he doesn't know what he'd need to do to fire up a landscaping or surveying company.

I don't know the first thing about starting up a landscaping or surveying company either.

But, you know what? There are *TONS* of successful landscaping and surveying companies here in Edmonton. There's probably a bunch of them where you live as well.

I asked him, "Why don't you call up a successful landscaping or surveying company, talk to the owner, and invite him out for coffee? Then, when you're with him, ask him if he'd be willing to tell you his story and ask him what he did to get to where he is."

There are two main reasons why most of us wouldn't think to do this:

1. We're scared that he will say "no" because he's too busy.

2. We're scared that he wouldn't agree to do this because he wouldn't want any more competition.

This might be the case for a few out there. But, I've spent a lot of time hanging out with business owners, and let me tell you they'd rather spend time teaching you how to avoid the same mistakes they've made than watch you fail.

Most business owners actually love telling their success stories.

And, they won't be afraid of you competing with them. But, just to be safe, you could call up a company in another city and drive out there to meet them for coffee.

Do you know what doing this does for you? It forces you to find a mentor.

I don't know a lot of successful people who did not have a mentor. Most of them followed the advice of someone else who got to where they wanted to go.

If you're a clerk, but you want to become a successful internet marketer, find an internet-marketing mentor. If you want to become a real estate investor and learn how to buy real estate with no money, again, find a real estate-investing mentor. And do everything he or she says.

You can pay for a mentor. That's a possibility. If you do, though, remember to do a bit of background checking first before you hand over any money.

Otherwise, offer to take someone out to coffee or lunch. Someone who already did what you're eventually hoping to do.

But, remember, it's up to you to actually do the work you need to do to get to where you want to go.

As mentioned previously, Tony Robbins has a pretty famous quote:

"Success leaves clues."

And the clues aren't even that hard to find; you just need to know where to look, and you need to be willing to follow them.

If you aren't currently working at your dream job, here's what I want you to do: Think about what you'd rather be doing. It can either be a better job or owning your own business.

Next, I would like you to find someone who's currently doing what you'd rather be doing, and ask them out to coffee or lunch.

I know this isn't an easy task but, remember, if you want to have something you've never had before, you need to start doing things you've never done before.

The worst thing they can say is "no." But, if you've heard me speak before, you may remember me mentioning that Jack Canfield's best-selling book *Chicken Soup for the Soul* was rejected by 154 publishers and Colonel Sanders' fried chicken recipe was rejected by 1,089 restaurants. You just need to keep asking until you find someone who says "yes."

Here's What Successful People Focus Most of Their Time and Energy On

Here's a question for you: What do you spend most of your time and energy focusing on?

As I've discussed, a lot of my mentors — Jack Canfield, Bob Proctor, Raymond Aaron — as well as other *New York Times* best-selling authors like Tim Ferriss, don't watch the news at all.

Most people are shocked when I tell them this. It's like we've been conditioned since birth to watch the news every night.

But, here's the thing: Most news agencies in the Western world are owned by private companies.

And . . . do you know the mandate of most private companies?

To make the most amount of money possible for its shareholders.

The more people that watch a certain news broadcast, the more money that particular media company makes.

So . . . the object of the game is to get as many people as possible to tune in, and not to provide us with the "news that matters most" as we are led to believe.

Here's another fact about the news: It's catered towards people who don't lead successful lives.

Successful people are interested in things like personal development, spiritual development, learning, teaching, innovating, and making the world a better place.

Unsuccessful people are interested in things like tornadoes, plane crashes, forest fires, celebrities, and traffic.

So . . . if you truly want to be successful, what should you spend your time and energy focusing on?

Yes, you should focus on things that matter, but there's more to it than simply that.

Now, the things that matter are things that affect your happiness, your health, your wealth, your family, and your ability to reach your goal.

Let's say that your goal is to quit your current job and get rich by starting your own internet dating site.

Here are examples of things that would then matter:

- YouTube videos on copywriting and internet marketing.
- The psychology behind matchmaking, dating, and healthy relationships.
- The hours of your favorite gym.
- The availability of your mastermind partners, accountability partner, and your mentor.
- The amount of money in your bank account.
- How-to books on building websites, driving internet traffic, and search engine optimization (SEO).

Note: A mastermind partner is a business buddy. This is a person with like-minded interests with whom you can brainstorm ideas, seek or give guidance, and get or provide support.

Now, let's talk about everything else — things that don't matter or things that have no bearing on your happiness, your health, your wealth, your family, or your goals.

Here are examples of things that shouldn't matter:

- Wars on the other side of the planet.
- The outcome of the game last night.
- Weather anomalies on the other side of the country that have no bearing on you, your target audience, your friends, or your family.
- What the president in another country is saying or doing.
- Opinions of others who are not experts helpful in getting you towards your goal.
- Opinions of random people on the internet who are not experts in any field that matters to you.
- What a certain celebrity says or does.

Now, let's talk about the things you can control. Remember, there is much more out there that we can't control than there is of what we can.

But, if you can't control something, why worry about it?

Here are examples of things that you *can* control:

- Your physical condition.
- How many times you meditate.
- How much money you make.
- Your mood.
- Your thoughts.
- The images you hold in your mind.
- What TV shows you watch.
- Who you hang out with and what you talk about.
- Books you read and courses you consume.
- How much you know about building a website.
- How much you know about driving traffic to your website, specifically people interested in internet dating.

Now, here's the last question, and it should be an easy one: Should you spend your time on things that matter or on things that don't matter? Remember, things that should matter are the things that improve your happiness, your health, your wealth, your family, and help you achieve your goals.

So . . . here's the key takeaway:

Focus your time and energy on things that matter and things you can control.

Anything else, no matter how captivating, is a waste of your time and energy. Most frustration and anger stems from trying to control something that is ultimately outside your ability to control.

So, don't. Don't try to control such things, and don't waste precious time worrying about them. Don't let things like terrorism or plane crashes that have no bearing on your friends or family affect you. Focus on what matters, and focus on what you *can* control.

And, if you haven't already tried this, try not to watch the news for a week or two. If you really need a news fix, ask a friend what's been going on. It's weird — news broadcasts normally last an hour, yet most people can sum up the previous night's news broadcast in 30 seconds or less.

Try it. Ask a friend what's been happening in the news. I'll bet you that his or her response won't last more than 30 seconds.

Get the Life You Want by Answering This Simple Little Question

A couple of years ago, Jack Canfield, founder of the *Chicken Soup for The Soul* series, asked me the following question:

"Do you take one hundred percent responsibility for your life and the results you're currently getting?"

At the time, I couldn't say "yes." I blamed my mom and my brother for forcing me to work at the miserable job I had at the time, and I blamed my friend for giving me some suspect stock advice — even though it was me who physically bought the stocks with my own money. At the time, I truly believed my mom, my brother, and my friend were the reason I didn't have the life I wanted.

Jack's words changed my life. His question inspired me to start becoming accountable and responsible for my actions and my results.

I got out of my brother's basement, moved in with my fiancée, and got a better job working fewer hours — along with a 50% pay increase. I even started buying investment real estate. Then, I married my fiancée, bought our dream house, had a baby, and started a few businesses. I even wrote two books and found a publisher, as well as writing my third book which you now hold in front of you.

Before I met Jack, I used to spend time with people who weren't happy with their life or their job. We would spend our time talking about TV shows we were watching or complaining about the economy. Stuff we had no control over.

Now I spend my time with best-selling authors, movie stars, and Olympic gold medalists. I spend time with successful people. We spend most of our time talking about how we can help others and make the world a better place.

Why was I able to turn my life around?

I took 100% responsibility for my life and my results.

I dispensed with blaming, complaining, justifying, and making excuses. I took 100% responsibility for the job I had, the income I was earning, and where I was living.

Then I decided I didn't like any of it so I got a better job, income, and home.

Even if I wasn't in control over my family's thoughts, opinions, or actions — or my friend's ability to pick stocks — I was still in control of my life. I was still in control over how much money I earned, who I dated, and where I lived. I just hadn't come to that realization before.

Even if I were to have gotten fired, I would still be in control over whether I could find another job or start a new business. If I had no idea how to get hired or launch a successful business, I had the option to engage an experienced mentor or coach to help me get to where I wanted to go and help me avoid costly and time-consuming mistakes.

So, let me ask you the same question: Do you take 100% responsibility for your life and your results? Don't worry if your answer is "no." I couldn't say I was either, at least not until a few years ago.

Ninety-nine percent of us don't take responsibility for the results we're currently getting in our lives. That's probably why most of us have neither the job, the income, nor the free time we want. That's probably also why 10-15% of us live beneath the poverty line even though — if you reside in the United States, or here, like me, in beautiful Canada — we live in one of the richest countries in the world.

Maybe your goal isn't to be the next President, the next Pope, or the next CEO of Microsoft. But, if you want to save more money than you're currently saving, build more wealth than you currently have, and experience more happiness and joy than you're currently experiencing, you need to start taking 100% responsibility for the choices you make and the results you get from those choices.

I understand that there are a lot of things that could happen to you that are completely outside your control. You can't very well control whether your company does a round of layoffs or even goes out of business, for instance.

But you can control how you react to such occurrences. You can decide to blame, complain, and make excuses for why you haven't found another job, or you can decide to do what you need to do in order to find another similar job — or to find entirely different ways to make money altogether, since there's more than one way to skin a cat.

Speaking of money, you're even in control over how much of it you make. It's true, even if your boss can't afford to give you a raise.

There are lots of ways for you to make some extra money while you're working at your current job. You can do network marketing. You can buy real estate to rent out to other people — even if you don't have any money or credit. You can make hair clips, coasters, or even jewelry to sell on Kijiji or Craigslist. I met a guy at my book launch, for instance, who buys ATMs and makes passive income from withdrawal fees!

Though I don't necessarily recommend it, you can even take a second job.

In order for you to get better results from your efforts, get a better job, or get more vacation time, you need to understand that you are responsible in attaining all that. It's not up to your boss to give it to you — it's up to you to ask for it. And, if he says "no," then it's up to you to keep asking. Or ask what you'd need to do in order to get what you want. Or, if you have to, find a new job. You can also just do nothing, but all that would accomplish is to create resentment — it wouldn't get you what you wanted.

Once I realized this, my life completely turned around.

I really hope that you can take this to heart and start working towards having the life, job, and income you truly desire.

Section Three: Overcoming Rejection

Why You Need to Treat Negative Feedback as a Gift

There's this one guy on my floor hockey team who's always saying something negative to his teammates about their play. I'll refer to him as "Tommy," though of course that's not his real name.

Tommy had it in for me in particular one morning at practice. All I heard for the better part of an hour was:

"Dan, you ****ing suck!"

"Dan, try harder!"

"Dan, don't do that!"

"Dan, stop giving the ****ing puck away!"

Not to brag or anything, but I'm actually pretty good at floor hockey. Just not at running. I'm admittedly the slowest guy on the floor, but once I have the puck — and I have a clear shot at the net — I'll score nine times out of ten.

Anyway, some of my teammates ignore Tommy. Others yell back at him. What do I do? I say, "Thanks for the feedback, Tommy." That's it. Nothing else.

There's a huge problem in our society right now: For every compliment we give someone else in our lives, we'll give them, on average, seven pieces of criticism or negative feedback. *SEVEN*. Worse yet, that number shoots up to *TWENTY-FIVE* or more when it comes to our self-talk. We'll give *ourselves* twenty-five pieces of negative feedback before we give ourselves a compliment.

But, while we don't have full control over what other people say, think, or do, we *DO* have control over how we *react* to what other people say, think, or do.

What do I mean by this? I mean that when most of us receive negative feedback, we take it personally. We let it hurt out self-esteem and our ego. And we'll try to justify our actions in response, attempt to shift the "blame" over to someone or something else, or just completely withdraw and apologize profusely.

But, here's the thing: There's this formula $E + R = O$, where:

E = Event

R = Your Response

O = Outcome

Most of us just let $E = O$. We let negative feedback and negative self-talk dictate our outcome — feeling hurt — instead of consciously thinking about and reacting to the feedback first.

Maybe Tommy was having a bad morning that day at practice. Maybe he was frustrated at himself about something he did earlier and this was his way of expressing his irritation. Maybe he's just jealous of the fact that I can score well and he can't. Then again, maybe he's just a jerk.

I don't know. But what I do know is that:

We need to treat negative feedback as a GIFT.

. . . no matter who or what provides it to us. After all, it lets me know I need to do something different. It lets me know I need to change the way I do something or the way I provide service to others.

For example, let's say a woman I'm trying to impress has thrown a drink at me. It happens. Not to me, of course. But, you know, hypothetically. Anyway, instead of getting all defensive and calling her all sorts of unpleasant epithets, I should treat her drink-throwing as a gift. A wet, messy gift, to be sure. But, still, a gift. I would replay the previous few minutes in my mind in an effort to figure out what *not* to do with the next woman I go out with, so I don't get another drink thrown in my face. Hypothetically.

How do you react to negative feedback?

I know it's tough to take sometimes, and it's easy to have the urge to get defensive or to try and find someone else to blame things on. But remember, if you want to grow as a human being, and you want to eventually get the income and lifestyle you've always wanted . . .

You need to take 100% responsibility for your life and your outcomes. There are no exceptions.

So, the next time you receive negative feedback from someone else, see if you can try to treat it as a gift. It's up to you to decide whether to use it or not, as not all advice will be useful in helping you get to where you want to go and attain what you want to achieve.

Don't Let This Stop You From Fulfilling Your Life Mission

I'm starting to see more and more photos on Facebook of couples in restaurants glued to their iPhones.

The photos are typically captioned with something like this:

"They spent their ENTIRE date on their phones! Isn't that sad? Look what society has become."

You know, I used to be one of those people. Not the ones glued to their iPhone. I mean I used to judge others who spent most of their time stuck to their iPhones during family dinners or during playtime with their kids.

But, as time went on, I started realizing the negative impact that judging others was having on me.

Why should I care what other people are doing? Are they threatening my happiness, my health, or my wealth?

No?

So, why should I be so concerned about what other people do on their phones?

Here's the thing:

Everything we judge in others is something we don't want to face within ourselves.

Smartphones are here. Most of us are going to spend some of our free time on them to varying degrees. It's just the way things are right now.

So... if you find yourself judging others for being superglued to their phones, take a look at yourself first. Is the problem related to how much time others spend on their phones, or your feelings towards others who, from your point of view, spend too much time on their phones? Perhaps you see a little bit of them in yourself, spending too much time on your *own* phone?

Well, there are only three things you can control:

1) The thoughts you think.

2) The images you hold in your mind.

3) The things you do.

You can't control how much time others, especially strangers, spend on their phones. So why waste your mental energy dwelling on them?

Do the work. Sort yourself out, and get to the point wherein the couple's actions no longer bother you.

Passing judgement on others, as well, puts you in a negative vibration. It does very little to help you get the lifestyle and income you want.

By the way, if they'd actually wanted to be talking to each other, the couple probably already would've been. If we didn't have such a thing as smartphones, they'd likely be having their dinner in complete silence.

At least now, with smartphones, they have something to do!

Section Four: Boost Your Self-Esteem

The 5-Minute Phobia Cure

During Rachel's delivery, I was scared of what was soon to come. I was scared of not knowing what to do. I was scared that I wouldn't be a good enough father for her. I was scared that I would accidentally hurt her or feed her the wrong food or change her diapers the wrong way.

I was trying to calm myself down by taking deep breaths and telling myself it would all be *OK*. After all, my job at that moment was to be there for my wife and help her in any way I could during the delivery.

But how could I do that while I was panicking?

I suddenly remembered a 5-minute phobia cure I learnt from a professional speaker a few years before. I tried it out, and it worked. I was much calmer, and I was able to focus my wife and help her as best I could during the delivery.

Do you have any fears or phobias? Do the thoughts of job interviews or performance evaluations frighten you? Are you afraid that with this current weak economy, perhaps you might be laid off?

If so, there's a very quick and effective way of overcoming these fears and feelings of anxiety.

When I first came across this technique, I didn't believe it would work. I thought that the only way of overcoming my fear of heights and my fear of large crowds, for example, was to force myself to look out the window at the very top of a tall building, and to force myself to walk through the most crowded area I could think of — a busy train station.

Unfortunately, that tactic didn't help. If anything, it made my phobias worse. The only thing I accomplished that way was to confirm to myself that, yes, I was indeed afraid of heights and afraid of large crowds.

But then I tried this 5-minute cure and my fears, feelings of anxiety, and phobias just disappeared.

The 5-minute cure involves tapping certain parts of your body while you're imagining what you're afraid of.

How To Perform The 5-Minute Phobia Cure

On Yourself

1. While thinking about the very thing that's causing you to feel scared or afraid, tap the fleshy part of the outside of your wrist (the "Karate-Chop or KC point) quickly thirty-five (35) times.

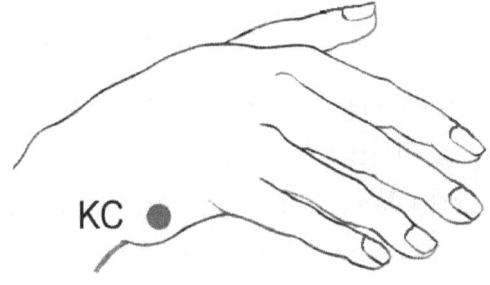

(Source: EMOFree.com)

2. Next, tap the top of your head (TOH) five (5) times.

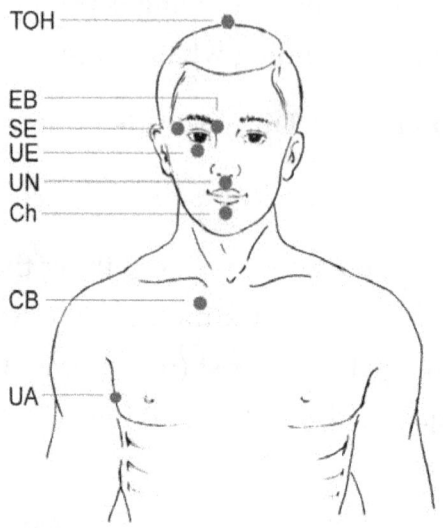

(Source: EMOFree.com)

3. Next, tap your eyebrow (EB) five (5) times. It doesn't really matter which eyebrow you tap. Remember to keep thinking about the thing that's causing you to feel scared or afraid.

4. Continue on with:

- The bone beside your eye (SE)
- The bone 1 inch under your eye (UE)
- Under your nose but above your lip (UN)
- Your chin (Ch)

- Your collar bone (CB), and

- On the side of your body, approximately four (4) inches below your armpit, at a point even with your nipple (if you are a man) or in the middle of your bra strap (if you are a woman).

If you find you're still feeling a bit anxious after performing the exercise above, try doing it again. Feel free to use your other wrist, eyebrow, collarbone, etc. the second time through. Keep going through the exercise above until you feel comfortable and at ease.

If you've tried this a few times and it's not working for you, you don't have to keep doing it. You don't have to keep doing something if you've tried it a few times and you're not getting the results you want.

But it worked for me and it worked for everyone I know who's tried it.

Remember, if there's something in your life that you don't like, you don't have to endure it. Do something about it. If you look hard enough for a solution, you'll eventually find it.

The Power of Celebrating Even the Tiniest of Successes

I took my wife and daughter shopping for clothes the other day.

While I was waiting in the changing room area while my wife was trying on a blouse for the 15th time — Honey, if you're reading this, you looked so beautiful in each and every one of those blouses! — I overhead a conversation between another mom and her 4-year-old boy. From what I could gather, she was trying to get him dressed.

It sounded like the little boy was able to put his shirt, shorts, socks, and jacket on correctly.

However, he apparently mixed up his shoes and put them on the wrong feet.

I'm sure you can agree that the little boy dressed himself pretty darned close to perfectly — and did impressively well for a 4-year-old.

But, here's the thing: What do you think his mother told him?

If you guessed, "Great job for getting dressed almost all by yourself!"

... you would unfortunately be wrong.

This is what I heard:

"You put your shoes on the wrong feet."

How do you think the little boy felt? Yup, not too good. I'm sure that statement didn't do much for his self-esteem or his self-confidence.

He got 4 out of 5 things exactly right. If he were in school, that'd be a mark of 80%. That's nearly good enough for an "A" in most places.

But the little boy probably wasn't feeling like he got an "A." He likely wasn't thinking about how good of a job he did putting on his shorts, shirt, socks, and jacket, either. Rather, he was made to think about his "failure" at putting on his shoes correctly.

You know, lots of high-ticket coaches have told me to overpraise and under-criticize. I highly suggest you adopt the same philosophy, especially in thinking about yourself.

Your inner chatterbox can be pretty dangerous if it's focusing on what you're doing "wrong" rather than on what you're doing "right." If it's only focusing on the one mistake you've made rather than the 4 things you did correctly, it's not doing any favors for your self-image. And it's going to inhibit your ability to go after the things you want in life and to help others in this world who really need your help.

Whenever you succeed, make a big deal out of it. Because it is. We want more of it. Whether it's waking up on time or landing a large media interview, celebrate it!

If you focus on what you did wrong, you'll lower your self-esteem — meaning you'll be prone to making even more mistakes.

The confidence boost you'll get from celebrating your successes will help you do an even better job next time.

How to Boost Your Self-Esteem Using Eye Contact

I've observed that people who don't have much self-esteem tend not to make a lot of eye contact. You can notice them as they walk around the mall or the office. They won't make eye contact with anyone.

I used to be the same way back when I had very low self-esteem.

So, here's my tip and homework for you: Take a stroll around the mall or the park by yourself, and make it a point to look 5 different people in the eye as they pass you by — or you pass them. That's it.

I'm not asking you to strike up a conversation with random strangers. Just walk around and try to make eye contact. If they look back at you, smile. They'll likely smile back — and trust me, that's an amazing feeling.

Don't break eye contact first. Wait for the other person to break eye contact. But, please don't beat yourself up if you do find yourself breaking eye contact first. It's OK. Just keep this in mind and please treat yourself gently. Commend yourself for taking action and working on this exercise in the first place.

Do this every day for a week.

Next week, try making eye contact with 10 people a day for seven days. Again, if they look back at you, smile. And, make it a point not to break eye contact first.

Completing this exercise will significantly boost your self-esteem. Also, any social anxiety you may have had will all but disappear. It's an amazing exercise that even I'll still do occasionally.

Boost Your Self-Esteem With This Bizarre Exercise

As we discussed a few chapters back in the previous section, for every 1 compliment the average person receives, they'll receive 7 pieces of negative feedback. This means that your spouse, your coworker, your kids, even your boss, will criticize you or provide you with negative feedback 7 times as often as they give you a compliment.

No wonder divorce rates are around 50%!

But that's not even the worst news. Again, it's worth repeating:

*We criticize **ourselves** 25 times as often as we compliment ourselves.*

What do you think that does for our self-esteem?

Substance abuse is at an all-time high. So is obesity. Alcohol consumption is nearing an all-time high as well.

The cause of all this? Low self-esteem.

Our happiness levels are lower than ever. Which is really very sad because we live in one of the most prosperous nations in the world.

How can we focus on helping others and living the lives we want when we can't even help ourselves?

Here's the thing: Who do *you* think is responsible for your happiness? Your family? Your spouse? Your pet? (that's why you have your furry little friend, right?) *Me?*

If you guessed "me," well, I will try to help you of course —that's why I wrote this book — but if you guessed "yourself," then you're correct. Ultimately, it's up to you to make sure you feel loved and appreciated.

If you're relying on your parents, boss, spouse, or partner for love and approval, I hate to say it, but it's not going to work. You can't control what someone else does or how they feel. But what you *can* control are your own feelings, thoughts, and actions.

It's up to *you* to make sure *you* feel happy, loved, and validated.

It took me 32 years to realize this. But it'll only take you a minute to give yourself all the love and validation you'll need to dramatically boost your self-esteem and your feelings of self-worth.

I'm going to teach you a technique. It'll seem bizarre at first. But, keep in mind that many success trainers as well as the world's best athletes do this on a regular basis.

It's called the "Mirror Exercise," and here's how you do it:

Please note: Before you do this, if you live with other people, tell them ahead of time that you're going to talk to yourself in the mirror so they don't think you've gone mad as a box of frogs.

Okay. So right before you go to bed at night, stand in front of the mirror and gaze at yourself.

Compliment yourself out loud for everything you've accomplished that day.

Then, say, "[*your name*], I love you." Then gaze at yourself for a few seconds and appreciate the image in the mirror.

For example, when I do the mirror exercise tonight, here's what I'm going to say to myself:

"Dan, you did an amazing job today explaining the mirror exercise to your loyal readers.

"Also, you did a wonderful job complimenting Kathy on coordinating that speaking engagement this weekend.

"Also, you did a fantastic job washing Rachel and putting her to bed.

"And, Dan . . . I love you."

This may sound like the most bizarre exercise that you've ever heard. But trust me, it works.

And it won't take longer than a minute or two.

If you're having trouble with self-esteem or you're going through a rough time right now, you need to do this exercise. It's no one else's job but yours to give yourself validation and approval.

It's not uncommon to feel a little awkward or uncomfortable when you do this, at least at first. It's very unnatural to compliment yourself in the mirror. That's because we're conditioned to put ourselves down, not compliment ourselves. But, try your best to power through. It'll be worth it in the end, believe me.

Lastly, I want to leave you with a wonderful quote I learnt from Meir Ezra:

"The key to success is overpraising yourself for even the smallest accomplishments."

Here's your homework: Do the mirror exercise tonight before you go to bed. Then do it tomorrow night. Then the next night. Then for the next 28 days.

Section Five: Overcoming Frustration and Anger

How to Release Yourself From Feelings of Frustration and Anger

Imagine you're driving on a two-lane highway. It's a bright sunny day, but the sun isn't shining directly in your eyes or anything so vision is completely unimpaired. It's 5:45 in the afternoon. The speed limit is 60. There are two cars in front of you, one in each lane.

Both of the cars in front of you are only going 35. And, they're driving right beside each other, side-by-side, so there's no way you can pass either one of them.

There are no traffic lights, intersections, or off ramps coming up for a while.

How do you feel? What thoughts are running through your mind? Frustration and anxiety? Thoughts like ...

"They should get off the road!"

"They should take the bus if they're scared of driving!"

"They should at least let me pass!"

"What's wrong with these people?"

"What are they thinking?"

"Are they even thinking at all?"

"Other people have things to do! Important things!"

"They're doing this on purpose, I know it!"

They are only going 35 in a 60 zone, after all, and for some reason they're not letting you pass.

This actually happened to me the other day. I was driving on a two-lane highway where the speed limit is 100 kph (60 mph). There were two minivans — I know, right? Minivan drivers are the worst — in front of me, both of which were only doing 60 kph (or 35 mph). I was also in a rush because Starbucks had half-priced Frappuccinos that day, but only until 6:00 pm. It was 5:45 and the exit to the nearest Starbucks was at least 10 minutes away. And I don't know about you but I really love Frappuccinos.

I used to have pretty bad road rage. I used to honk at cars going at the speed limit and I would prevent other cars from merging onto the highway if they weren't travelling at the speed I wanted them to go.

But, not this day. On this particular day, I was calm and relaxed, in spite of not being able to travel at the speed I wanted to go so I could make it to Starbucks in time.

Here's why: I used a technique I learnt from reading Byron Katie's wonderful book, *Loving What Is*.

Byron calls this technique "The Work" and it's comprised of three steps:

Step 1: Judge the other person.

> In this case, judge the drivers of both cars. They shouldn't be on the road if they're too scared to drive. They should both be in the right-hand lane. It's not fair to the other cars on the road who want to go the normal speed limit. The least they could do is let me pass.

Step 2: Ask yourself four questions.

Take each of the statements in Step 1 and ask the following four questions:

1. Is it true?
2. Can you be 100% sure it's true? — skip this question if the answer to question 1 is "no."
3. How do you feel when you think the thought?
4. Who would you be without the thought?

Let's apply the 4 questions to the thought, *"If they're going to drive slowly, they should let me pass."*

- Is it true? — Well, yes. There's this thing. It's called consideration.
- Can you be 100% sure it's true? — Well, I really want to think so, but who knows? Maybe they know something I don't and they're going slow for a reason. So, no, I can't be 100% sure it's true.
- How do you feel when you think the thought? — Stressed, annoyed, frustrated, and angry.
- Who would you be without the thought? — Much more relaxed and content. Even happy.

Step 3: Turn it around three times and discover how each turnaround is true.

The Work is based on the thought that whatever negative feelings or judgments you pass on others are actually a reflection of negative feelings or judgments you hold of yourself.

Once you realize this, you free yourself of negative feelings you hold towards other people.

There are three ways to turn around the judgment:

1. To yourself.
2. To the other person.
3. To the opposite.

Let's apply this to our example.

Original thought: *If they're going to drive slowly, they should let me pass.*

> ➤ To yourself.
>
> New Thought: *If I'm going to drive slowly, I should let myself pass.*
>
> There's nothing I can do about making the other two cars go faster. So, I need to let myself pass on these negative thoughts and emotions.

> To the other person.

New Thought: *If I'm going to drive slowly, I should let them pass.*

This one is tougher, but I need to discover how this statement is true. So, for me, for this example, I'm driving slowly. It may be because the other cars are driving slowly as well, but it doesn't change the fact. So, I should give the other drivers a pass and stop being annoyed with them.

> To the opposite.

New Thought: *If they're going to drive slowly, they should not let me pass.*

If they should let me pass, they would have. But they're not. So, they should not let me pass.

I credit the four questions and the three turnaround statements for eliminating my road rage tendencies. Slow cars no longer annoy me, at all.

And, this works for other parts of your life as well. Are you stuck with in-laws you don't like staying in your house? Judge them, ask the 4 questions, then turn the judgement around. If you still have lingering negative feelings, redo the process until they're gone — the negative feelings, not the in-laws!

I mentioned earlier that only you are responsible for how you feel or what you think about. If you're starting to get frustrated with someone else, you're focusing on them. If you're focusing on them, who's focusing on you? Once you turn around your negative feelings and judgements and start focusing on yourself, you'll feel a *HUGE* sense of release — and relief. It feels amazing knowing that no one can say or do anything to make you feel negative feelings or think negative thoughts.

So, here's your homework:

Think of a reoccurring stressful situation in your life. Next, fill in this sheet. Then do the work on it.

Section Six: Money

How to Earn More Money Without Getting a Raise or Working More Hours

You can always earn more money.

No, I don't mean by "getting a second job" or by "finding a higher-paying job."

I mean by setting up:

Multiple sources of income.

Real Estate is one way to do it. Buy a property and rent it out. There are even ways of buying real estate without using any of your own cash! I won't go into it here, but there are *PLENTY* of people out there who can show you how to do just that.

How about selling stuff on amazon and eBay? Lots of people do that. Even Gary Vaynerchuk himself.

Note: Gary Vaynerchuk is an American serial entrepreneur whom I admire — a four-time New York Times *bestselling author, speaker, and a leading wine critic who grew his family's wine business from $3 million to $60 million.*

Yes, once in a while, even someone like Gary will head out to a garage sale and sell some of the stuff he buys on eBay for a hefty profit.

You could get into Affiliate Marketing. This is where you sell stuff for other people. Like, if you sold my books for me and I gave you 50% of each sale, for instance. You would have a product to sell, and I would have someone selling my stuff for me.

If you worked really hard at it, you could make a living as an affiliate marketer — I'm talking $10,000+ per month.

I have multiple sources of income. I have real estate and book sales, but I also market personal development products.

Here's my point: If you're low on money, there are literally *TONS* of ways to get more of it. You just need to go out and do it. Find something to sell, and sell it.

Look around. You could join a Network Marketing program — as long as the products they sell are legitimate — or, you could sell your skills on Craigslist or Kijiji.

Maybe you work in an office, but you love fixing cars? Post a classified. Offer to fix other people's cars in the evenings and on weekends.

Money problems can be fixed; you've just got to hustle.

You know, you could also try something like selling t-shirts online.

You could target a group of people with a common interest, say truckers in Denver — yes, I'm stealing this example from Gary Vaynerchuk's latest book *#AskGaryVee*.

What are the chances that a trucker from Denver would want a t-shirt that says *"Denver Truckers Rule!"*?

You can actually get a pretty nice t-shirt design from *fiverr.com* for $5, upload it to *teespring.com,* and have them drop-ship t-shirts to your customers for a cost of around $10 a shirt. Charge your customer $20 for a t-shirt and make them pay for the shipping as well.

Oh, how do you find Denver truckers? You can run an ad on Facebook that targets people who are from Denver who list their occupation as *Trucker* — or who are married to truckers, or who are related to a trucker.

If you run your advertisement properly, it shouldn't cost more than 20¢ to get a potential customer to click on your ad.

See, there's a money-making idea right there. But it requires some time and effort on your part.

This Message Could be Worth $3000 to You (Especially if You're a Landscaper)

The other day, when I took my wife and daughter out for a stroll, I noticed our neighbor had a sign on their lawn which said the following:

ABC Landscape Company

XXX-XXX-XXXX

Call for a free estimate

Note: to protect the business, I'm not going to use the actual name of the landscaper.

The first thing I thought when I saw the sign was, *"Free estimate? Isn't that redundant? Who charges for an estimate?"*

Now... let's pretend you're ABC and by luck someone actually saw the number on your sign and decided to call you. Yay.

Why would they call you? Well, there's a very good chance they're looking to hire a landscaper.

But, guess why they're *actually* calling you. Yup, they want to know how much you cost.

They're price shopping. They're going to call all the landscape companies in your city and pick the cheapest one which still has decent online reviews.

So, where does that leave you?

Well, you're going to have to sell the caller on the fact that you're cheaper and better than all the other landscapers out there. Which means you'll need to over-deliver on razor-thin profit margins or you won't be in business for very long.

Now... let's assume you hire me for an hour of consulting and I tell you to make a few minor tweaks.

What if I had you change the wording on your signs to:

Call XXX-XXX-XXXX
For a FREE

Consumer Awareness Guide to Hiring a Landscaper

Now, how many more calls do you think you're going to get?

Yeah, yeah, they're just calling because they want the free guide, but stay with me here . . .

When they call you and ask for the free guide, just send it to them! No questions asked. Don't try to sell them anything — yet!

What you want to do is attach a personalized cover letter — addressed to the prospect by name — outlining what the prospect will find in the guide. Also, you'll want to send them a small inexpensive token, like a petunia. Yes, still for free — stop being so greedy!

Now, in this letter, offer the prospect a free "Landscape Audit." What the prospect will get with a Landscape Audit is an hour of your time where you visit their house, and make some suggestions on how they can improve the look and feel of their yard. Let them know what the life expectancy is of the stuff they currently have —flowers, shrubs, trees.

If they've never had any landscaping done before, do a layout plan for them.

Now, *after* you've overwhelmingly impressed your prospect, you can *then* ask for the sale.

See how much better this is than just asking them to call for a free estimate so you can go to their house and ask for the sale?

How about taking it one step further?

Go to houses that look like they need landscaping, drop off a free petunia and a free *Consumer Awareness Guide to Hiring a Landscaper*. Then, offer them a free Landscape Audit!

How long does it take to write a consumer awareness guide for landscapers? Just put together 3 or 4 articles on what consumers should look for and what they should avoid when choosing a landscaper.

Here are a few article suggestions:

- *3 Questions You MUST Ask Before You Hire a Landscaper*
- *The Difference Between Price and Value*
- *Watch Out for These 5 Landscaping Rip-Offs*
- *How to Get a Landscaper to Guarantee Their Work*

If you are indeed a professional landscaper, you should be able to put this guide together rather easily.

Making sense?

Give, give, *GIVE* . . . then ask for the sale. And when you *DO* get the sale, over-deliver.

By the way, if you *are* a landscaper, you can make my $3,000 consulting fee payable to *Dan Christian Yeung*. Just kidding, of course. Unless you really want to pay me. Then I'm totally not kidding.

Seriously, though. Don't forget: *Dan Christian Yeung*.

The Middle Class is Disappearing: Make Sure Your Money Doesn't Follow Suit

I was chatting with a stranger on the elevator the other day. I asked her how she was doing. She said she was happy because it was Friday and that she "didn't have to work tomorrow." She then asked me if I was glad that I didn't have to work tomorrow either.

I told her I work every day of the week.

Note: my email subscribers may well have noticed this, since I'll regularly email them even on Saturdays and Sundays.

She was bewildered. She asked me what it was I did for a living.

See, that's a hard question for me to answer, because I don't just do one thing for money — I do lots of things. I have real estate, I do private lending, I authored a couple of books, I do contract work, I do affiliate marketing, I'm in the process of testing and launching a new job-placement business...

But, here's the thing: I *LOVE* doing this stuff.

Remember earlier in the book how I was talking about the difference between successful people and the rest of us? Here's another one:

Successful people only do what they love.

And there lies the rub: The reason most of us are glad when it's Friday and we don't have to work the next day is because we don't like what we do. We spend most of our waking hours working a job we don't like to do for someone we don't like doing it for. And we spend most of that time being worried that we'll be fired or laid off.

I'm sorry, but this is crazy.

You should love what you do. You should be excited to wake up and go to work because the stuff you do for work energizes you and gives you a great deal of satisfaction.

In fact, if you love your work, you can hardly call it "work" at all. But if "work" is indeed all you do, then you're not going to have a particularly enjoyable life.

See, I *LOVE* giving back. I love helping others improve their lives and their self-esteem.

So, how do you get to this point? How can you do only what you love while making money at it?

Most people get hung up on the second part — the "make money doing it" part — and then they stop focusing on the first part, which is to do only what you love.

Here's the thing about making money, though: Most people only have one source of income — their job. This is probably the case for you.

But, here's the thing about wealthy people. To reiterate:

Most of them have multiple sources of income.

Rather than focusing their time and energy at a job, they focus on spending their time trying to create a source of passive income that they don't have to actively manage. And, once it's created, they try to create another. And another. Once they create enough, they go on a trip to Panama.

And, here's the thing: Because they set up multiple sources of income, they come back from their vacation even richer than they were before they left. Isn't that ridiculous?

So, how do you set up multiple sources of income?

I'm glad you asked.

One of the easiest ways is to lend your money to someone else. You can do this through companies such as Paramount Equity or ProFunds.

Another option, if you have enough money for a down payment for a property, is to buy investment real estate and collect money from your tenants. If you don't have enough money for a down payment, guess what? You can still buy investment real estate! You can borrow the money from someone else, or you can even borrow the money *FROM THE SELLER!* If you're interested in learning more about this, email me at *danc.yeung@gmail.com*. I'll show you how to get started.

You can also learn how to do internet marketing. One book to start with is *Multiple Streams of Internet Income* by Robert Allen.

You can even do network marketing, though I'd be *VERY* careful which network marketing company you decide to join. Some of them have *AMAZING* programs, but others are really shady.

So, here's your homework: Think really hard about whether you actually love doing what you're doing for money right now. If you do, awesome! If not, think about what you'd *rather* be doing for money. Now, think of something you can do *RIGHT NOW* to get you on your way to making that money by doing what you actually love.

Next, start learning about passive income. I talk extensively about passive income in my book *Save Money, Build Wealth*. Buy it on Amazon or book a free coaching session with me by emailing me at:

danc.yeung@gmail.com

... and I'll be happy to give you a copy along with the session.

Don't want to take my word for it? Buy *Multiple Streams of Internet Income* by Robert Allen or borrow it from your library and read it. Alternatively, start watching videos on YouTube that discuss passive income. Just open the YouTube app on your phone and search for "Passive Income."

The gap between the wealthy and the poor is growing at an astronomical pace, and the middle class is starting to disappear. Please, I urge you to consider setting up multiple streams of income now. If you have any desire to secure a comfortable retirement, this is an absolute must-have.

The Ancient Babylonians Were a Very Wealthy Race: Want to Know Their Secret?

It's a very common problem in our society: Most of us don't have enough money to do the things we want to do.

For some reason, we're always short on cash. If you were having money problems 10 years ago, there's a very good chance you're still having money problems today.

People are always asking me: How can I make more money? What's the one tip you can give me that will dramatically increase the amount of money I have in my bank account?

I tend to disappoint a lot of people with my #1 tip. Most people want to hear about a crazy investing strategy or an amazing business opportunity that will make them a zillion dollars in a matter of hours.

But, there's a problem with that . . .

Let's say that you currently make $70,000 a year, but you also spend that $70,000 on things like your house, taxes, car, food, vacations, eating out, etc. You tend to not have any money left in the bank at the end of the year.

Now let's say that you win the lottery. You win $15M. Bam. Congratulations.

You're not used to having $15M in the bank. You're used to earning $70,000 a year and spending it all. So . . . what do you do?

You start buying stuff. It'll start with paying off debt. Then it'll be a bigger house. Then a better car. Then a yacht. Then you buy your friends stuff. Then . . .

Did you know 70-98% of lottery winners declare bankruptcy within 7 years?

I've studied the teachings of many financial gurus such as Robert Kiyosaki and I've also studied unconventional investing, and buying investment real estate with no money down.

But, do you know what most financial gurus say is the #1 key to achieving financial freedom?

For every paycheck you get, pay yourself 10% of it FIRST.

Notice that I'm not saying, "Save 10% of your income." I'm saying pay yourself first. Before you start giving money to the rental company, the mortgage company, the car loan company, the grocery store, the movie theater, etc., give some of it to yourself *FIRST*.

Sixty-two percent of us have less than $1,000 in savings. Not very sexy, is it? Yet, for a lot of us, this is our normal.

The reason we're so broke is because we're too focused on giving our wages to other people and we forget to give some of it to the most important person in our lives: *ourselves*.

The Ancient Babylonians were a very wealthy race. I don't want to turn this into a history lesson, so I'll spare you the details, but Babylon was one of the richest empires to ever exist.

Want to know why they were so wealthy? George Samuel Clason said it well in his best-seller *The Richest Man in Babylon*:

"Ten percent of all you earn is yours to keep."

Don't do it last. Pay yourself first. Get into this habit.

If you aren't currently doing this, do you think it's something you can try? Just try it for a couple of months. Make it a point to move 10% of your paycheck into your TFSA (Tax-Free Savings Account) or your Roth IRA the second you're paid, then try to figure out how to make it through to your next paycheck with the remaining 90%.

If you find a way to make this work, and you do this consistently over a span of decades, you'll have more than enough money for a comfortable retirement.

Why You Always Have a Choice (Even When It Feels Like You Don't)

A few months ago, I gave a listen to a new personal development podcast series.

The episode I listened to consisted of the host interviewing an ostensible personal development guru. The guru seemed to know what he was talking about. He even wrote a book on the subject.

Though, even with his apparent credibility, he made the following statement:

"There are times in life where we have a choice, and other times where we just have to cope with what life gives us."

Cope?

He cited a hypothetical example wherein, if your boss asked you to stay an extra 30 minutes after work to complete a task for him, you'd have no choice but to "do what he said." If you were efficient with your time, you could conceivably get away with only having to stay an extra 20 minutes, but you'd still have to "cope with your boss's decision."

Dude. Really?

If I'd been conducting the interview with the guru, I would've responded with the following question:

"So, Mr. Guru, what would happen if this person were to say 'No' to their boss's request?"

The answer would probably have been:

"You'd look bad, you could get reprimanded, and you could possibly even be suspended or fired."

Then I'd say:

"So, you're *choosing*, then, between working late, or ruining your reputation, or maybe even getting fired."

See what I mean?

No matter what, unless you're in jail or in a country run by a very hands-on dictator, you'll always have a choice. You might have to choose between something bad and something worse — like between staying in an abusive relationship or dealing with a breakup — but it's *still* a choice.

And, trust me, you'll feel a lot better knowing you always have a choice no matter what. Even if it's between two undesirable outcomes.

The SWAT Team and Your Life Mission

About a year ago, a SWAT team — a tactical unit of elite police who specialize in high-risk tasks such as hostage rescue — was called in to close down the street right beside my office. A guy was sitting on the ledge at the top of an office building. He was thinking of jumping, it appeared, but obviously he hadn't jumped quite yet.

Life must have been pretty bad for him right then, or at least that's the way it must have seemed from his point of view. Something terrible might have happened for him to consider such a drastic measure as to take his own life. Maybe he'd just gotten laid off. Maybe his girlfriend had just dumped him. Or, maybe someone really close to him had just died.

But, here's the thing: Life is precious. As far as I know, we only get one ride on this merry-go-round. I've read a bit about reincarnation, but no one's convinced me yet that they've come back for the 21st time.

Life is a gift. You have to treat it as such.

Most life forms on our planet have been gifted by The Universe with a physical body.

But, The Universe also gifted us with a great intellectual capacity and a spiritual soul. Not all life forms on this planet get this — only us humans do. Okay, supposedly dolphins are pretty smart or whatever. But all they ever do is swim in the water and eat fish, so . . . I'm sticking by my claim.

As humans, it's our duty to express our gratitude to The Universe for this amazing gift.

How?

By figuring out why we're here, what our life mission is, and to ultimately fulfill it.

How do you know what your life mission is?

Look back on your life. What kinds of things did you do that gave you joy? What are you most passionate about?

Earlier that day, I'd asked my friend this exact question. After a bit of thought, she realized that she absolutely loves interior decorating. She loves giving people advice on what furniture and drapes they should buy, and she also loves helping people design their floorplans. Not only does she love this, but it's her true passion. In essence, it's her life mission. The Universe put her on this planet to help other people live in more attractive and comfortable homes.

Do you know how exciting life becomes once you discover your life mission? Life takes on a whole new meaning. You start to realize that your life isn't only for you. You realize that you are here to help and serve others by doing what you absolutely love to do.

How is she pursuing her passion? Well, right now she isn't. She doesn't know how to start. Needless to say, I got her to commit to calling interior decorators and home builders and to offer to take them out for coffee (refer to my earlier chapter in Section Two).

What about the guy on the roof? Well, he's also got things he's really good at and things that he absolutely loves to do.

He also has a life mission. We all do.

But, it sure isn't to jump off a building.

If he dies, the rest of us lose out. We lose out on his talents and gifts.

He was in a really negative vibration, there's no doubting that. The world from his point of view did not look attractive at all.

But, here's the thing: He, and he alone has the power to change that.

There are only 3 things we have control over as humans:

1) The thoughts we think.
2) The images we hold in our mind.
3) Our physical actions.

He obviously had negative thoughts hanging around in his mind. I know it's tough to do when you're in a really negative vibration, but you need only to start thinking about and visualizing things that give you joy. Think about the things you're really passionate about.

Start looking for things to be grateful for.

You'll get out of your negative vibration very quickly. And, all of a sudden, you'll start to see that the world we live in is full of possibility.

Fortunately, the police were able to coax the jumper-to-be away from the ledge.

Section Seven: Goal-Setting and Achievement

How to Achieve Any Goal You Set for Yourself

My friend, Jeff, regularly attends high-ticket real estate investing seminars. I'm talking $225 for a three-hour seminar which happens 4 times a year.

The point of attending these seminars is so that you can learn how to buy expensive property without any money. But, it seems like they focus more on goal-setting than anything else.

At least two of the three hours are spent on reviewing previously set goals, setting new goals, and sharing the new goals with the other attendees.

I asked Jeff if people were *actually achieving* their goals. He said, "No, not at all. It's a waste of time."

It's not that uncommon, really, for people to fail to achieve the goals they've set for themselves.

When most people set a goal, they just write something down. Something like: *I will clean the house, I will lose weight,* etc. You might have even heard that when you set a goal, you're supposed to use the "S.M.A.R.T.E.S.T." method.

If you haven't heard of SMARTEST, here's what each of the letters mean:

Any goal you set needs to be…

Specific

Measurable

Achievable

Realistic

Timely

Engaging

Shifting

And you need to have a **T**eam helping you.

Just because your goals conform to the SMARTEST method of goal setting doesn't mean that you will achieve them, necessarily.

And, when it comes time for you to review your goals and you realize you haven't reached any of them, you won't feel very good about yourself. Feeling bad about yourself isn't going to help you grow as a person — it's going to hinder it.

But what if there were a means by which you could set a goal in such a way that you could achieve it, no matter what, as long as you put in just a little bit of effort?

Guess what? There *IS* a way to do just that.

Instead of just setting a goal, set three levels of achievement for each goal you set. Let's call these levels "Minimum," "Target," and "Outrageous."

➤ **The Minimum Level** of the goal you set needs to be very attainable and needs to be achievable with little to no effort.

➤ **The Target Level** of your goal is the meat of it and should be just beyond your reach.

➤ **The Outrageous Level** of your goal is way beyond your reach and it would be crazy if you were to achieve it.

So, for example, let's say that my goal was to clean my house. If I were to use the SMARTEST method, my goal would probably look something like this:

I will clean all the rooms in my house and garage, put everything away, and sweep and vacuum all the floors by the end of the day on April 30, 2016, so I can feel happier and more comfortable in my house. I will get my wife to help remind me to do this.

Here's what my goal would look like using the MTO method:

> Goal: I will clean my house by the end of the day on April 30, 2016.
>
> - o Minimum: I will clean the earplugs off my nightstand.
> - o Target: I will sweep and vacuum the floors and put everything away.
> - o Outrageous: I will hire a cleaning company to come and clean my house and the garage.

So... how do you get the motivation to achieve your *T* or even your *O*? By doing your *M*. Once you do your *M*, you'll have the motivation to go after the *T* and the *O*.

John C. Maxwell has an amazing quote which explains this beautifully:

"The whole idea of motivation is a trap. Forget motivation. Just do it. Exercise, lose weight, test your blood sugar, or whatever. Do it without motivation. And then, guess what? After you start doing the thing, that's when the motivation comes and makes it easy for you to keep on doing it."

Even if I were to just achieve my Minimum, I would feel much better about myself than if I were to set a huge goal and not achieve any of it. It feels a lot better to achieve at least part of your goal, even if it's the easiest part.

Next time you want to set a goal for yourself, or your boss is making you do it as part of your performance evaluation, MTO the goal. If all you do is reach your minimum, you've already achieved your goal. The T and O are just gravy at that point.

If you haven't achieved at least your Minimum, it's very likely because you didn't get around to even attempting to achieve your goal in the first place.

So . . . MTO!

How to Get Motivated to Do Something You Don't Feel Like Doing

It can be tough to get motivated to do something you don't really want to do, especially on a Friday afternoon when the weather outside is really nice.

This goes for just about anything, from mowing the lawn, to working out.

I love this quote from Bob Proctor, considered by many as the father of personal development:

"Start doing the thing to have energy to do the thing."

It's kind of counter intuitive, right? You need to *have* the energy and the motivation to *do* the thing — like go for a run — before you can actually *do* the thing.

But here's what Bob Proctor and many other experts on procrastination and motivation suggest:

Just do a little bit.

If you want to motivate yourself to use the treadmill that's sitting idly in your basement, just go stand on it for a minute every day for a week. You don't have to turn it on or anything. Just stand on it.

After a while you'll find the energy to turn it on and start walking. And then you'll find the energy to turn the speed up and you'll find yourself running.

There are many other examples. Need to vacuum the house? Just go plug the vacuum in. Don't do anything else. After you plug it in, you'll find the energy to vacuum a room. And then another room. And then another.

How about mowing the lawn? Just wheel the lawnmower outside. Don't start it up.

Need to study for that test? Take your binder out of your backpack and open it. Don't do anything else.

Next thing you know your lawn will be mowed and your nose will be buried in your notes.

Don't believe me? Try it! Think of something you've been putting off for a long time. Now, think of the very first step you'd need to take in order to get the task accomplished — standing on the treadmill, changing into your painting overalls, finding your doctor's phone number, or what have you.

If you don't find yourself completing the whole task, that's OK. Try just doing a little bit again tomorrow.

Tomorrow, go stand on the treadmill, change into your painting clothes, or look up your doctor's phone number.

Try this every day for a week, or until you find yourself running on the treadmill, painting the entire fence, or booking an appointment for your next checkup.

If after a week's time it's still not working, stop doing it. Chances are, though, that you'll start finding the energy to work on tasks for which you've long been procrastinating.

Either way, let me know how this little technique works out for you.

The Rule of 5: How to Get Huge Tasks Done Faster Than You Think

Have you ever been faced with a *HUGE*, daunting task? By this I mean setting up a website with your own domain, repainting your entire house, or renovating your basement?

I spoke in the previous chapters about ways you could motivate yourself to complete a complex task. This involved starting out with a very simple task you can complete to get you on your way to finishing the rest of the project. By doing that simple task, you'll find the energy to keep going and do other tasks you need to do to accomplish your goal.

But what if that doesn't work?

Well, I have another suggestion. This is a technique I learnt from *The Success Principles*, written by Jack Canfield, again, founder of *Chicken Soup for The Soul*. It's called:

The Rule of 5.

Basically, what the Rule of 5 states is that if you have a huge task you need to complete that will take a long time for you to do, instead of focusing on the entirety of the task, just do 5 things each day which will get you that much closer to completing your objective.

So, let's say that you need to cut down a tree by swinging at it with an ax. I know this doesn't sound like a lot of fun at all — unless you're a lumberjack — but, what if you went out and just took 5 swings at it? Then, the next day, you went out and took another 5 swings at it. And then the next day. And, then, the next...

Eventually, even if it took 100 days, that tree would come down.

Note: I don't mean empty swings. You actually do have to hit the tree. And remember, also, when swinging axes around: safety first!

Now, as for your basement renovation. Instead of focusing on every single thing you have to do all at once, why not start by simply planning where everything is supposed to go. Then, the next day, clean the basement out. Then, the day after, start tearing apart a few rooms. If you focus on just doing a few tasks each day, then eventually you'll have a brand-new basement.

Note: Do not use the axe to tear apart your basement area. It's important to use the right tools for the job and also you are not Jack Nicholson in The Shining. *And remember: safety first!*

So, here's what I would like you to do: Think of a huge task you need to do at some point, one you've been putting off because you're afraid it's going to take forever to get done. Now think of 5 things you can do to get started, and actually do them. The next day, go do another 5 things. Do another 5 things the day after.

Before you know it, you'll have that huge task that you thought you'd never get around to doing done.

How an 81-Year-Old Bob Proctor Can Still Crush It Onstage Like He's 20

You're probably familiar with the words "comfort zone."

It's the zone where you, well, feel most comfortable.

Your comfort zone is dependent upon and governed by the thoughts, habits, and beliefs you currently have.

Your daily routines, where you get your daily coffee, the salary you earn, the shows you watch on Netflix, the people you hang out with ... these are all elements of your comfort zone.

This also applies to your health and your finances. You have the amount of money you have in the bank right now because you're comfortable with that number. Same goes for your salary. If you wanted more money in the bank or a higher salary, you'd work tooth and nail to save as much as you could and/or get a better job or start a business.

But, if you did all that, you'd be venturing out of your comfort zone into unfamiliar territory.

Same with your health. If your goal is to lose 50 lbs., once you've lost the weight — unless you did some work on your subconscious mind as well — you'd be out of your comfort zone. Unless you see yourself as worthy of your new body, you'll gain back the weight just as quickly as you lost it.

Most of us spend 99% of our time and energy within the confines of our comfort zone. And, if by chance we find ourselves slipping out of it for a second or two, we hightail it right back in.

Why? Because slipping out of it is uncomfortable. We don't like to feel uncomfortable — we prefer to feel comfortable. That's why we have big-ass leather couches and recliners pointed towards our 72" TVs. That's why most of us don't like change.

But, if you're reading this, you're probably looking to improve your income and/or your lifestyle.

Well, if you want to do this, you'll have to get used to venturing outside your comfort zone.

There are three zones you can be in: Comfort, Performance, and Danger.

Growth doesn't occur in your comfort zone. It occurs in your performance zone.

But, here's the thing: We're constantly in motion. The cells in your body are always vibrating.

Has anyone ever told you they "don't have any energy"?

The notion that you don't have any energy is somewhat erroneous.

You have enough energy in your body to power half the country even when you're dragging ass!

Even when we pass away, our bodies are still in motion. If they weren't, our bodies would turn to dust the moment we passed.

We also grow when we exercise our bodies and our mental faculties. When we exercise our bodies, we get stronger. When we exercise our mind, our memory gets sharper and our intuition becomes more acute.

So, if we're always in motion, that means we're never

staying still.

When you stay in your comfort zone, however, you're not growing. Since it's impossible to stay still, guess what happens?

Yup, you're disintegrating. Your body starts to shut down, and your mind begins to weaken.

That's why you'll see people who retire at 65 pass away just a few years later. And, that's why you'll see a 70-year-old Raymond Aaron and an 81-year-old Bob Proctor still crush it on stage like they were 20.

Get out of your comfort zone. Get used to being in your performance zone. You don't have to be in the danger zone — unless you're Kenny Loggins or Archer — but do get out of your comfort zone!

If you want to grow as a person, if you want to improve your income and/or your lifestyle, you'll need to get used to being in your performance zone. That's where growth happens.

And, try not to use the word "uncomfortable." Get it out of your vocabulary altogether! Use the word *unfamiliar* instead. Most of us would rather be in an "unfamiliar" situation than an "uncomfortable" one.

Success Leaves Clues — Do You Know How to Find Them?

The other morning, I found myself in the middle of a conversation with a would-be entrepreneur. He was telling me all about his dream of one day opening up a coffee shop.

I responded with, "Wow that's awesome! So, what are you doing right now to make it happen?"

He was speechless. He didn't know what to say.

As I've mentioned, Tony Robbins is famous for saying, "Success leaves clues."

But what does that mean, exactly?

Well, whatever it is you want to do, and you really want to succeed at, there's probably a good chance someone else out there has already done it. And not only done it, but absolutely nailed it on the noggin'.

I gave my new aspiring-entrepreneur friend the following advice:

First, get in contact with the owner of a popular coffee shop in your town.

Then, ask them if you can buy them a cup of coffee. Yup, it's the old invite-them-for-a-cup-of-coffee routine again! Come to think of it, they probably already have plenty of coffee, being a coffee-shop owner and all. But that's okay. Improvise! Invite them to lunch. Or invite them for a beer or two.

Whatever you invite them out for, tell them you really admire what they do and what they've accomplished, and that you're thinking of running a coffee shop yourself. Tell them you would really appreciate it if they could spare a few minutes to chat with you about their journey.

Once you have the meeting, make it all about them. People *LOVE* talking about themselves and their successes.

Ask them how they got started. Ask them what they love most about it!

Keep in mind, they're doing you a *HUGE* favor by sharing their valuable time with you; you have to treat it as a gift and be very grateful for it.

You'll eventually learn how to get started in the business. Or, you might learn that it may not be a business you'd want to get into after all.

Also, if you'd like, you can even ask the other person if they'd be willing to be your mentor. Ask them if it's OK if you kept in touch. All you really need is a few minutes of their time every other week or two.

If you're worried they may say "no," remember that most entrepreneurs — at least the good ones — would rather help you succeed, especially if you're right in their wheelhouse, than watch you fail.

And if they do say "no," find another person to ask. How many successful coffee houses are there in your town? If there aren't a lot, drive to another city and look for one. Don't just daydream about *"how nice it would be if you could own your own coffee shop."* Get in motion!

So, this fellow was very grateful for my advice, and he agreed to ask 5 different coffee shop owners if they'd be willing to have coffee or lunch with him.

Did he actually go through with it? I don't know. I never did get his contact information. But I can tell you, if he's not willing to get into action, his dream of one day owning his own coffee shop will forever remain a dream.

Why You Can't Go at It Alone

One of my friends is thinking of buying an investment property here in Edmonton. He's thinking of using money from his RRSP — Registered Retirement Savings Plan, similar to a 401(k) — to fund his purchase.

But, here's the thing: He's not 100% sure what the tax implications would be.

Will he have to pay tax on the money he's taking out of his RRSP? Or, can he take advantage of Canada's Home Buyers' Plan where he can borrow money from his RRSP to fund the purchase of his first home, even though he's using the money to buy an investment property?

I personally don't know the answer. But, there's someone on my team who does. I referred my friend to one of my real estate-investing mentors, someone who specializes in creative financing.

Every successful real estate entrepreneur I know has surrounded themselves with a very competent team of associates. They're aided by very good accountants, realtors, lawyers, and assistants.

Actually, I don't know a single successful entrepreneur who doesn't have a team of coaches, assistants, lawyers, and accountants. And, many of them have partners that complement their experience, knowledge, and skill sets.

Success is a TEAM sport.

Who's on your team? Do you even have one?

We're all very competent in a few areas. Some people are very gifted at reading through legal contracts. Others are talented at negotiating the purchase price of a home.

But if we're only very good at a *few* things, that means we're not very good at everything else!

Is that a bad thing? *NO!*

But, it means that if you desire success, you'll want help. You'll need to find other people to be a part of your team — people who have the skills and expertise you require.

Remember, though, that people care mostly about their *own* needs. So, although you'll benefit from finding people who are willing to join your team — and who have expertise you wish to make use of — you have to understand they care primarily about what's in it for them.

Ideal partners and team members will ultimately have *their* most important interests and requirements fulfilled by providing you with the expertise *you* need — a mutually beneficial relationship!

Have you asked a few people to coffee or lunch as I proposed in previous chapters? If so, listen to them. I'd be willing to bet they'll tell you they didn't get to where they are all by themselves. Whether it be their family, their friends, or the staff they hired, they had help.

Even successful internet entrepreneurs have teams. Virtual assistants cost much, much less than you'd think — so it makes sense to have them do some of the repetitive work.

Who's on your team? Who's helping you get to where you want to go?

If the answer is *"no one,"* I suggest you make an effort to find a mentor. This is vital. Find out what kinds of people they surrounded themselves with when they were first starting out.

Also, remember that you have the option to use a Virtual Assistant to do online tasks such as: send and answer emails, book appointments, look for and analyze properties, transcribe audio recordings, run ads on Facebook, and all kinds of other stuff!

I highly suggest you visit *taskbullet.com* and see what they have to offer. Their VAs only cost about $5-$10/hr.

Remember, no one gets to where they want to go all by themselves. Neal Armstrong wouldn't have landed on the Moon without a team of scientists and engineers behind him. A 62-year-old Raymond Aaron wouldn't have been able to hike 350 miles in minus-50-degree weather to the North Pole without the aid of trainers and navigators. Even figure skaters, boxers, and tennis players have a team of nutritionists, trainers, and coaches behind them.

If you don't know anyone offhand who'd be willing to be on your team, go look for them! Go to *meetup.com* and look for groups of like-minded people. Network. Participate in online forums and Facebook groups. Get in motion!

Are You Still on Track?

If you've been reading through my books and blogs, you've probably done a few of my exercises in service of your life mission. If so, awesome!

But, here's a question: *How often are you doing this?*

When you start doing things like:

- joining a mastermind group
- getting an accountability partner
- writing daily articles
- meditating and visualizing
- repeating affirmations
- creating vision boards
- getting good-quality training

... you *change* as a person.

When I say "change," I'm really saying *grow*.

The world starts making more sense to you. Things become clearer. Once you sort out messes and open cycles in your mind and in your environment, you gain clarity.

So, in the midst of all this changing and growing, do you think it would make sense for you to revisit your life mission?

It might still be the same as it was before. But, I'm willing to bet it's evolved a bit.

See, the thing is, as much as I want to help you, ultimately, you're the only person who can figure this out.

Only you can discover your life mission.

Not me. Not a $50,000 coach. We can help you navigate your mind, but we can't discover your life mission for you.

So, it's up to you to routinely check in with yourself to make sure you're still doing what it is you're meant to do.

When I first started on this journey, for instance, I thought I wanted to make lots of money investing in real estate. My heart was telling me I hated real estate, but I ignored what it was saying to me. Who wouldn't want to own every single apartment building in the world and make tons of money?

When I finally started listening to my heart, however, I thought it was telling me to help others buy cars at dealerships without getting ripped off.

I still enjoy doing that but, about a year ago, I realized my heart was telling me that my ultimate goal was to help people like you get the life you've only ever wished of having.

I meditated earlier today, in fact, and realized this is still my life mission.

Check in with yourself. Do it every few months or every year.

Is your life mission still your life mission?

How to Navigate Through Tough, Life-Altering Decisions

Have you ever been confronted with a genuinely difficult decision you had to make?

For example, have you ever wondered if you should marry a certain person that you really like, but you're not 100% sure that you want to spend the rest of your life with them?

With friends and family putting loads of pressure on you, would you honestly be able to figure out what your heart really wants?

It's a tough question to answer.

Last night, I was visiting my friend Jeff. Jeff is considering having a new house built for his fiancée and himself. He even has a floor plan picked out.

However, he's not actually 100% sure he wants to go ahead and have the house built.

His mind is telling him *yes*. But, he doesn't know if it's because it's actually the right move, or if it's just because he's infatuated with the thought of having a brand-new house.

To help him answer this question, I introduced him to the Sway Test.

The Sway Test is an amazing tool that you can utilize to ask yourself what your heart really wants. Sometimes it's tough to drill all the way down through to your heart and your subconscious mind. Limiting thoughts, beliefs, and fears easily get in the way and cloud our thinking. We usually end up picking the easiest option, even if it's not exactly what we truly want.

After doing the Sway Test, Jeff discovered that he indeed truly wanted to get a new house, but not necessarily at the price the builder was asking him to pay.

Jeff felt a huge sense of relief once he had his answer.

Next time you're faced with a difficult life-changing decision — such as whether or not you should have a baby, or change your career — and you're afraid that you won't be able to be objective, try the Sway Test. It will tell you what your heart really wants.

I'm very grateful that I was able to help Jeff, and really hope this will be of help to you as well.

The Sway Test

Get into a comfortable, balanced standing position. Don't put yourself right up against a wall since, for the purposes of this test, your body is meant to sway either forwards or backwards depending upon the results of the test.

1. Relax, calm yourself, and breathe in and out. You want to be grounded, and yet light within your own center of gravity. You want to avoid being stiff or rigid here. Let your body be supple.

2. Take your hands and place them together over your chest.

3. Focus on the proposition in question. Let that thought fill your mind and body. Try not to introduce any bias or undue influence into the test. Just

relax, fill yourself with the desired thought, and let your body do as it will.

4. Notice which way your body moves, or have an observer notice this for you.

Analysis:

> A forward sway means the proposition in question is beneficial for you and/or what your heart desires.

> A backwards sway means it is detrimental for you and/or *not* what your heart truly desires.

> No sway at all — no detectable movement — means neutral.

Try it yourself!

What Would Your Life Look Like if You Asked Yourself These Three Questions?

Most people know Bob Proctor as one of the stars of the movie *The Secret*.

Again, Bob is considered by many to be the father of personal development. He's written heaps of books and he's taught loads of courses on wealth and personal growth.

He's helped thousands of people become multi-millionaires in only a matter of years through the benefit of his personal-development coaching. He's also helped businesses to double their profits in a matter of mere months. The Prudential of America, one of the largest insurance companies in the world, credits Bob for increasing their profits by hundreds of millions of dollars in only a year.

He even helped Sir Edmund Hillary to become the first person ever to climb to the top of Mount Everest.

I love listening to him speak and coach. His techniques are nothing short of amazing. They're so simple, yet they can change the course of your life or your business.

I wanted to share one of his techniques with you today. It's a really simple technique that he's advised countless times to dramatically increase the revenues and profits of the people and businesses that hire him.

It's a very straightforward technique. It involves asking yourself or your team three questions:

1) What are you doing?
2) What works?
3) What doesn't work?

Then, you stop doing what doesn't work and start doing more of what does.

It's so easy to get caught up in the tasks our boss delegates to us, and to not give too much thought to them once we're engaged in them. Sometimes we forget why we're even doing what we're doing.

It's the same with your personal life. You do things all the time that stop you from getting to where you want to go. But you won't know what these things are until you stop and ask yourself these three questions.

If you want more for yourself and your family than you currently have, you need to stop doing what doesn't work. Even if it's something you've been doing your entire life. Then, you need to figure out what *is* working and start doing more of that.

Bob tells a story of an engineering firm whose owner had just died. The owner left the business to his wife. Because she had neither business nor engineering experience, the people on the board of directors presumed she would almost certainly sell the company.

But, she didn't.

The first thing she did was call a meeting with the board of directors. Then, she asked the three questions. Lastly, she asked them how they could stop doing what wasn't working and start doing more of what in fact was.

The result? She increased the firm's yearly profits from $10 million a year to $25 million a year.

She didn't know how to run a business.

She wasn't an engineer.

All she did from then on was come in to the business 4 times a year to ask the board of directors these same three questions.

Imagine what *your* life would look like if you asked yourself these same three questions periodically.

These three questions are part of the reason I went from being broke and living in my brother's basement to becoming an award-winning author and having Bob Proctor come to my book launch.

Section Eight: Productivity

How to Conduct a Powerful and Productive Meeting

Have you ever been to a meeting which felt like a complete waste of time?

Well, I just came from one. We spent the entire meeting deciding whether or not we should have another meeting.

Yup. Seriously. I wish I were kidding but I'm not. We spent an hour on this one topic.

I'm willing to bet these types of meetings are actually fairly common.

And, the worst part is that once the meeting was over, a few of us stayed behind and had an actual productive meeting. And . . . *that* meeting only lasted 15 minutes!

You know, I was listening to an *@iLoveMarketing* podcast just the other day. The hosts, Dean Jackson and Joe Polish — two of the most brilliant marketing minds in this day and age — were interviewing Cameron Herold, founder of 1-800-GOT-JUNK. Apparently, Cameron's a genius at conducting productive meetings. So much so that he wrote a book on meetings called *Meetings Suck*.

Anyway, here are some suggestions and takeaways I got from this particular podcast:

1. Start each and every meeting 5 minutes early.

   Punctuality is important. Use motivation if you need to. You can show a funny YouTube clip right at the beginning of each meeting, or you can implement a rule where the last person to show up has to buy everyone else lunch.

2. End each and every meeting 5 minutes early.

   This ensures that most of the discussion that occurs during the meeting is on-topic and relevant to achieving the meeting objectives.

3. Schedule each and every meeting for half the amount of time you think you need.

   Same goal as the previous objective.

This also ties in to Parkinson's Law with states that, "Work expands so as to fill the time available for its completion."

So, if you think you need an hour to have a discussion, try scheduling it for only half an hour. You'll be surprised how efficient and effective your shortened meeting will become.

4. Always have an agenda and a note-taker.

   Having an agenda keeps the participants focused and motivated, especially if you cut the typical time allotted for such a discussion in half.

   Having a note-taker allows for the other participants to stay focused and engaged on the discussion rather than on their laptops or their notebook computers.

5. Know the objective of the meeting beforehand.

   If you don't know this, you're going to have a very sloppy meeting. Everyone who has a desire to contribute will contribute, but they're going to focus more on speaking their minds and offering up their opinions than on attaining the objective of the meeting.

6. Don't hold a meeting unless the decision-makers are present.

   This ties in to the previous tip – There's no value in holding a meeting if there's no way to achieve the objective. I've been to meetings in the past where the people that were there didn't have the authority to make the decisions that needed to be made in the meeting.

   If the objective of the meeting is to devise several options and find one to recommend, that's fine, but if a decision needs to be rendered, at least one of the attendees must have the authority to make that decision.

7. Ensure the most senior person speaks last.

   This way, everyone else at the meeting is able to share their opinion without being influenced by their supervisor's point of view.

8. Implement a give-and-take system for off-topic laptop and smartphone usage.

   Implement a system where if someone is asked to spin their laptop around or show their phone, and it turns out they're on Facebook or Instagram or Twitter, they have to buy lunch for everyone else at the meeting. Alternatively, if someone is "caught" but they're actually doing something work-related, then the leader of the meeting — the one doing the "catching" — has to buy everyone at the meeting lunch. It goes both ways.

And there you have it. Now, do you have to do absolutely all of this? Of course not! Do what works. Read this list, and take some of your favorite suggestions in to your next meeting and see if it doesn't improve your meeting efficiency.

Why You Can't Manage Time but You *CAN* Manage This

Bob Proctor likes to tell a story about a time he was invited out for breakfast by Earl Nightingale, the most listened-to man on the radio back in the 1950s.

Bob was always happy and grateful whenever he had a chance to be alone with Earl. He would pepper Earl with a well-prepared list of questions every time the two were together. Bob actually gave up a million-dollar business for an $11,000 yearly salary just to work in an office next to Earl.

On this particular morning, he asked, "Earl, how do you manage time?"

He could still hear Earl's fork hit the plate. "Nobody can manage time. Time can't be managed. What I do is manage my activities."

What a concept. Time can't actually be managed. There's nothing we can do to make it go faster or go slower. If we're having fun, time seems to go faster than it does when we're bored, but that's just an illusion.

So, how do you manage time in regard to your activities?

Well... I can tell you what Earl did. He wrote down what he needed to do on a sheet of paper and carried it around with him. Every time he completed or delegated a task, he crossed it out.

How simple is that?

How do you manage your activities? Do you keep a sheet of paper with you — or use an app on your smartphone — write down what you need to do, and just go do it?

I can tell you what I do, and it works for me: I write down what I have to do, but in three categories.

- ➢ Category 1: Do immediately
- ➢ Category 2: Do within the next 10 days
- ➢ Category 3: Do at some point in the future

I only look at the items in the third category on Monday mornings and will move an item up to the second category if I think I can get it done within the next 10 days. Next, I get all the items done in the first category before moving on to the tasks in the second category.

I based this system on information I got from Michael Linenberger's excellent book, *Master Your Workday Now!*

How do you manage *your* activities? Do you use a calendar? A to-do list? I suggest you try out Michael Linenberger's system for a week or two and see how it works for you. I can tell you, before I discovered Tim Ferriss' system, I was using Michael Linenberger's and I was able to double my productivity. Now, I use a combination of the two.

By the way, Bob turned Earl's simple idea into a product that he was able to sell for millions of dollars.

How to Make It Harder for Your Boss to Lay You Off

A few weeks back, I overheard a couple of people chatting on the elevator about how work was going for them. One was scared that they were going to be laid off because of the slowing economy here in Alberta.

As I got off the elevator, I realized that the Law of Compensation isn't a really well-known law.

If you're not familiar with it, here's what the Law of Compensation states:

Your compensation will always be in direct relation to:

1) The need for what you do.

2) Your ability to do it.

3) The difficulty there is in replacing you.

There's likely already a huge need for what you do, or else you wouldn't be making money at it in the first place. If there wasn't a huge need for what you do, you wouldn't be doing it or getting paid for it. So, #1 is already taken care of. I'll talk about #2 in a second. Concerning #3, however, if you get *REALLY GOOD* at what you do, you'll become very hard to replace. Especially if you can ramp up your efficiency and the quality of your work.

So... how do you increase your salary at work and reduce your chances of getting laid off? Get really good at your job. You have to admit this statement makes a lot of sense even if I weren't referring to the Law of Compensation.

Luckily for you, not a lot of people put much effort into getting better at their jobs. So, if you take a few courses a year and increase your productivity by 20% or more, you'll stand out in a very positive way.

By the way, this also applies if you're an entrepreneur.

But, how do you get better at your job?

This takes us back to point #2 in the LoC. You can *ALWAYS* improve your ability to do what you're currently doing, and to do it particularly well. You can continually find more effective ways of doing your current job more efficiently. The best way to do this is to engage in regular training pertaining to your area of employment. For instance, if you're a structural engineer, take structural courses and attend structural and architectural conferences on a regular basis.

How do you improve your efficiency? The quickest and most effective ways I know are to read Tim Ferriss' *The 4-Hour Workweek* and Michael Linenberger's *Master Your Workday Now!* and apply the techniques found within. Get them on amazon or borrow them from your local library.

I'll give you a very quick tip I learnt from *The 4-Hour Workweek*:

Only answer your emails and voicemails twice a day at most. Otherwise, keep your inbox closed. I suggest checking it at 11:30 am and 4:00 pm if you work a 9-5 job. And, before you start responding to your emails, open up *e.ggtimer.com* and set it to 5 minutes. Then answer your emails as fast as possible. You'll be surprised as to how efficient you all of a sudden become once you use the timer.

And, most people won't really mind if you respond to their email 3 hours later instead of right away.

If people generally like to fire emails right back at you after you send a response, and you'd like to alleviate having to deal with that, if you use Gmail, then add Boomerang. Boomerang allows you to delay sending emails for a few hours or so. That way you can respond to an email at 4:00 pm, but the email won't actually be sent until, say, 6:00 pm.

Here's another quick tip: When you answer the phone at work, instead of saying, "How are you?" say, "How can I help you?" This will cut the amount of time you spend on the phone in half.

If used properly, these tips could add several hours' worth of productivity to your workday, thereby making you much more efficient. And this means you become more valuable and harder to lay off.

But, remember, you actually have to take action. Read these books I've mentioned and put the stuff you learn to use!

How to Find an Extra Seven Hours a Week of Free Time

I was having coffee with my friend the other day. He spent most of the time complaining about how he doesn't have a lot of free time. He went on and on about how he wished we had more than 24 hours in a day.

The first thing I asked him was, "How much time do you spend watching TV?"

After thinking about it, his answer was, "Four hours a day."

He then justified it by saying that he *has* to watch the news and HGTV every day because he's a real-estate investor.

I then asked him, "If you had to cut out one hour of TV, what show would you not watch?"

He was able to answer this one rather quickly. Apparently, if you watch two different shows where two different ordinary families learn how to buy investment property from two different "gurus," watching a third show following a third couple learning how to buy investment property from a third "guru" doesn't really add all that much value.

Anyway, four hours a day may sound excessive, but sadly my friend is not in the minority.

The average American and Canadian watches FIVE hours of TV a day.

This means we spend roughly 35 hours a week in front of our TVs. That's very nearly the equivalent of a full-time job!

Just to put this in perspective, the average college or university course requires 3 hours a week of classwork. Assuming the standard course load is 8 courses a semester — 24 hours a week — then in four years you could complete an entire degree with this time and still have 10 hours a week to watch your favorite shows.

Imagine what spending five hours a day in front of the TV is doing to your mind and your body.

Do you know the first piece of advice Jack Canfield's mentor, W. Clement Stone, gave to Jack? He told Jack to watch one less hour of TV a day. Not cut it out completely, but just watch one hour less.

Jack asked Clement what he should do with that extra hour.

Clement told Jack to do whatever he wanted. He could go for a walk or a run. He could spend the extra hour with his wife or his kids. He could learn a new language. But, the best usage of that extra hour according to Clement was to read a non-fiction book, preferably one that would teach him a useful skill, or to read an inspiring biography.

How much TV do *you* watch? If it's more than an hour or two a day, how would you feel about following W. Clement Stone's advice? Do you think you could cut out an hour of TV every day, and spend that time exercising, spending time with your family, learning a new skill, or reading a non-fiction book?

When I tried doing this for the first time, I suddenly felt that I had much more free time. My relationship with my wife became stronger, and I've read more books in the past year than I did in the previous 30 years COMBINED. And I didn't miss that extra TV show I'd cut out one bit.

If you're someone who wishes you had more money, imagine what your financial situation would look like in a year if you spent seven hours a week learning about investing, marketing, and running a small business.

Remember, I'm not asking you to throw out your TV. I'm just asking you to cut out one hour of TV-watching a day.

You'll be surprised how much this will change your life.

Why Working on Your Weaknesses is a Waste of Time

I'm often reminded of a very typical interview question:

"What are some of your weaknesses?"

When I do interview coaching, I tell my clients to answer this question with something like "public speaking," and then give a list of what you're doing to improve upon it — "I joined Toastmasters, a debate club," this sort of thing Then, give the interviewer an example of a success you had after working on your "weakness" for a while — "By improving my communication skills, I was able to convince a potential investor to invest in our company," for instance.

But, here's the thing: Trying to improve upon your weaknesses isn't, as you might think, actually the best utilization or application of your time.

Raymond Aaron, *New York Times* top-ten best-selling author, has an amazing quote:

"If you spend your time and energy working on your weaknesses, you'll have many strong weaknesses."

See, there are things we're good at and things we love to do, but, there's also a much greater list of things we're not so good at and are not so keen on doing.

Successful people don't spend time, money, or energy on getting better at things they're not good at; they spend their time, money, and energy getting even better at the things they're *already* good at and the things they LOVE to do.

Think about it. Try to think of a successful person. You can go with a wealthy person like Bill Gates or Warren Buffet, or you could go with someone non-wealthy like Mother Theresa, Gandhi, or the Dalai Lama.

Do you think they got to where they were, or are, by "improving their weaknesses"? No, they got to the level of greatness they did by exploiting their strengths and letting others do the additional tasks that needed to be done.

Sure, they might have had to do a few things they didn't particularly like doing, but they spent 90% of their time, money, and energy doing what they loved to do and what they were good at.

The first thing people like to tell me is that they "can't afford to hire other people."

There are a few ways to address this:

1) Use a Virtual Assistant.

    As mentioned previously, VAs cost about $5-$10 an hour, and they can do things such as scheduling appointments, accounting, bookkeeping, internet research, and making online purchases. I'm currently using TaskBullet and I have nothing but positive things to say about them.

2) Find a neighborhood teenager.

    Post an ad on Craigslist or Kijiji, or respond to one, or simply ask one of the teenagers in your own neighborhood. Teenagers can mow your lawn, shovel your snow, or paint your fence. They shouldn't cost more than $5-$10 an hour, and they're happy for the chance to make some money. They need new video games, after all, or whatever it is teenagers do these days — who can truly say what teenagers do?

3) Barter.

Again, head over to Craigslist or Kijiji and offer your services in exchange for services you're looking to delegate. For instance, if you're an accountant, and you love to do accounting but you'd like someone to clean your house, offer to trade someone accounting services for cleaning services.

You can also find these services at networking events. Remember, you don't go to networking events to sell your stuff — you go to them to provide value to others and look for partners.

I used to go to lots of real-estate networking events, and there would always be contractors hooking up with realtors, lawyers, and interior decorators. They often ended up making *HEAPS* of money together flipping real estate.

Do you think the contractor would have done as well trying to be his own lawyer, realtor, and interior decorator?

I can tell you myself that I don't like managing my own rental properties. I don't like looking for tenants, doing background checks, and responding to inquiries in the middle of the night.

So, I hired a property manager. Sure, it's costing me money, but I have much more free time this way that I can then spend doing what I love to do and, in my humble opinion, what I'm good at — providing value to *you*.

I do not allow my employees to do anything they don't want to do. Everyone only completes tasks they like doing and things they're good at. Everything else gets done by an outside contractor. Let me tell you that this methodology alone creates an amazing and productive work environment.

Please keep in mind that I'm not asking you to all-of-a-sudden just cut out all the tasks you don't like doing.

Pick 2 or 3 things you don't like doing that a VA could conceivably be doing for you (scheduling appointments, applying for jobs, writing reports, etc.) then head over to TaskBullet and take a look at what they have to offer.

You *DO* Have the Time — You're Just Choosing to Waste It

I've had many people tell me how much they admire me. They admire the fact I've written a couple of books, invested in 6 pieces of real estate, and started two businesses. To top it off, I did all of this within the span of one year.

Then, they tell me they wish they could write a book or start a business like I've done, but they "just don't have the time."

Does this sound like you? Well, if so, then you may not like so much what I have to say next . . .

The truth is, even if you have kids and a full-time job, you *do* have the time to start and run a business. You're just choosing to spend it elsewhere on other things.

I'm serious.

Don't hate me!

I love you and I'm telling you this for your own good.

Honest!

Here's the thing: We all have the same 24 hours in a day. Let's say you spend 8 of them working and 2 more commuting to and from work. This leaves you with 14 hours.

Let's say you sleep for 8 hours a night, and you spend another 2 with your kids. This leaves 4 hours.

Four hours a day plus a $5 per-hour virtual assistant is *MORE* than enough time for you to run a business.

See, the problem isn't that you don't have enough time to run a business or write a book. Rather, the problem is that you don't want to give up some of the things you'll need to give up in order to write your book or run your business.

You don't want to give up watching *Game of Thrones* or *Walking Dead*. You don't want to give up watching hockey or football. You just don't. Otherwise, you wouldn't be complaining about "lack of time."

Okay, to be fair, not wanting to give up watching *Game of Thrones* or *Walking Dead* is completely understandable. But still. You get my point.

Gary Vaynerchuk preaches the 7 pm-to-2 am workday. You wake up, go to work, come home, and work on your business from 7 pm to 2 am.

Now, I've tried that. For me, it's too much. On weekends, I can stay up until 2 in the morning, but on weekdays, for me to function properly I need to go to bed at least by midnight.

But, here's the thing: I'm getting stuff done. I wrote my third book. I'm also working through two training programs — one on Neural Linguistic Programming and one on How to Become a Success Trainer.

All this while being an engineer. And, raising a daughter.

You can accomplish the same. If you're complaining that you don't have the time to do something you really want to do, then take a look at where you're spending your time. Are you watching the news? Are you spending half your free time on Facebook and the other half playing Slither?

If so, it's not that you don't have the time to build your business or write your book — it's that you're choosing, consciously or unconsciously, to spend the bulk of your time on your phone or in front of your TV.

Remember, if you're complaining about something, it means you have the power and ability to change it. If you didn't, you wouldn't be complaining about it.

Ever hear a hunched-over 80-year-old man complain about gravity? That's why he's hunched over. If it weren't for gravity, after all, he'd be able to stand upright. But you're not likely to see him cursing gravity, because what would be the point? It can't be controlled and it can't be changed.

If you have the urge to complain about something, why not first see if there's something you can do about it? And, if not, why not try doing The Work — the wonderful Byron Katie's exercise, discussed in Section Five — and see what you come up with.

Otherwise, it's fine to complain. Just remember that no one's forcing you to do anything. If you don't *think* you have the time to start working towards getting the lifestyle and income you really want, guess what? *You won't.*

On the other hand, if you truly want to find the time to work on achieving the lifestyle and income you really want, and you want to make the world a much better place in the process, *you'll find a way to do just that.*

Impress Potential Clients With This Memory Hack

I came across a cool memory hack the other day. It's a way to easily and instantly memorize a list of names or objects. This method doesn't require repetition or rote learning. All it takes is a bit of creativity.

When I met a potential client at a networking event, he couldn't stop talking about his four kids. It was obvious he loved them very much. So, I decided to test out the memory hack and see if I couldn't memorize the names of each of his kids while he was boasting about them.

It turns out this technique was much easier to use than I thought it would be. He only had to mention each of his kid's names once for me to remember them all.

His kid's names are: Sierra, Trudy, Palmer, and Kim.

How did I memorize their names so easily?

Well, here's what I did: As soon as he mentioned the name of one of his children, I quickly searched my mind for a person or object similar to the name.

The name of the first child he mentioned was Sierra. I immediately thought of the GMC pickup truck. Easy enough.

The name of the next child he mentioned was Trudy. I immediately pictured Rudy — the name of the main character in a well-known football movie — driving the GMC Sierra with his gold Notre Dame helmet on.

The next name he mentioned was Palmer. I imagined Rudy sticking his palm out, much like what football players do when they try to break a tackle — *Palm*er.

The last name he mentioned was Kim. I imagined Kim Kardashian sitting next to Rudy. Why? I don't know. But Kim K was the first image that came up in my brain.

So, here's my question to you: What's easier for you to remember?

Sierra, Trudy, Palmer, Kim

— or —

The image of *Rudy*, driving a *Sierra*, sticking his *Palm[er]* out, with *Kim* Kardashian sitting beside him.

I know it's a bit of a weird image, but it's how our brains work. Our brains aren't trained to remember raw data — they're trained to remember stories and images, especially ones that are atypical or unusual and stick out in some way. I highly doubt you're going to forget the image of Kim K sitting in a truck with Rudy sticking his palm out anytime soon.

Try this out the next time you're out at a networking function or you're meeting a potential client. Others will be extremely impressed with your ability to memorize their name as well as the names of their spouse and kids, and they'll be flattered as well that you did so.

Not only is this a good way to ingratiate yourself with potential clients, but this technique also works well if you're in school and you're studying for an exam.

How to Make Your Memory 100x Sharper

I recently came across a very impressive video on YouTube. A guy stood on stage and correctly memorized the order of a deck of 52 cards.

I have a question for you: Do you have a perfect memory? If you think you don't, then you're in the majority.

But here's the thing: According to Bob Proctor, lead teacher in the movie *The Secret* and, as I've said — and it's worth repeating — considered by many as "The Father of Personal Development" . . .

We ALL have a perfect memory.

If you don't think you have a perfect memory, it's probably because you don't exercise it often enough. Our minds, and our memory faculty, will easily deteriorate if we don't exercise them. It's just like the muscles in your arms. If you left one of your arms in a sling for a long time, the muscles would atrophy and your arm would become virtually useless. On the other hand, if you were to lift weights with the free arm, you'd build huge muscles in it.

Although your mental faculty isn't a muscle, it acts in much the same way in that, if you exercise your memory on a regular basis, you'll have a fantastic memory well into the latter years of your life. If you don't exercise it, on the other hand, you'll soon be complaining about your "poor memory" — if you aren't already.

Okay, on to how to make your memory 100x sharper . . .

Most people will tell you that you can improve your memory just by doing the following four things:

1) Exercise on a regular basis.
2) Exercise your memory on a regular basis.
3) Sleep 8 hours a night.
4) Eat healthy.

I'm going to show you an additional way to improve your memory. Let's say, for example, that for some reason you need to memorize this number:

4524985665

How would you go about doing this? Most people would start by memorizing the 4, then 4-5, then 4-5-2, then 4-5-2-4, then . . . well, you get the picture.

There are two issues with this method:

1) By the time you get to the 7th digit, you're going to start having a tough time.
2) This isn't all that fun, is it?

Let me show you a better way of doing this.

Our mind *LOVES* stories, senses, and images. It likes things that invoke strong feelings, whether it be funny, sad, erotic, or grotesque. It *HATES* raw data like letters, words, and numbers. And, it hates rote learning by repetition.

So, why don't we try telling a story with this number?

The first three numbers are: 452

Well, "four" sounds a lot like *door*, "five" sounds a lot like *hive* and "two" sounds a lot like *goo*.

So, let's start with this story:

You open the front door to your house, and you see bees in a beehive making goo.

Yeah, I get that this statement sounds weird, but stay with me.

The next three numbers are: 498

The next part of your story could then become:

You continue walking and see Thor sitting at a table with a blind date.

The next three numbers are: 566

So, the next part of your story could be:

You enter your kitchen and see a bird nosedive into a basket of bread sticks.

The last number is 5, so you could say that:

Lastly, you go into your dining room and see a live band.

So, what would be easier for you to memorize:

4524985665

— or —

You enter your front door and see a beehive of bees making goo. Next, you walk into your living room and see Thor with a blind date. Next, you go into your kitchen and see a bird nosedive into a basket of bread sticks. Lastly, you go into your dining room and see a live band.

Weird, eh? it's MUCH easier to memorize a story, even one that doesn't make any sense, than to try to rote learn a set of 10 consecutive numbers which don't have any meaning to you. It's a lot faster and much more enjoyable this way as well.

Another thing that I'd like to point out is that I had you go around in your house in your mind. Using this technique where you go around an environment you're familiar with makes it a much more powerful image, and hence easier for your brain to retain. I might also have asked you to go around your office or your childhood home, for instance.

Here's your homework: Come up with a random 10-digit number. Then, try to memorize it by making up a funny story using words that rhyme with the numbers you're trying to memorize. You can use *rhymezone.com* to help you out.

And, please, I urge you to exercise your memory periodically. An easy way to do this is to play a memory game on your phone.

Conclusion

If you're fortunate enough to have made it this far, you will have realized that you can indeed have anything you want in this life. Nothing is out of reach for you.

I only wish that some of the wisdom I've just shared with you over the past 200 or so pages could have been shared with you earlier on in your life, but at the same time I am truly grateful you had the chance to get your hands on this book, giving you the opportunity to change your life around.

May you live the rest of your life with an abundance of happiness, health, and wealth.

Love,

    Dan

About the Author

Dan Christian Yeung has committed his life to teaching you how to utilize his powerful goal-setting strategies and life-management tools in order to dramatically change your life for the better. Plus, using his own innovative techniques developed over the past decade, he shows you step-by-step how to take conscious control of your world so you can get from where you are to where you want to be.

Dan has spent many years developing, refining, and testing the techniques that he teaches so that you won't have to struggle to get what you want in life. You don't have to reinvent the wheel. You simply have to follow his guidance and benefit from the lessons he has learned.

They are his gift to you.

www.ingramcontent.com/pod-product-compliance
Lightning Source LLC
Chambersburg PA
CBHW070644160426
43194CB00009B/1566